Miniature Lamps

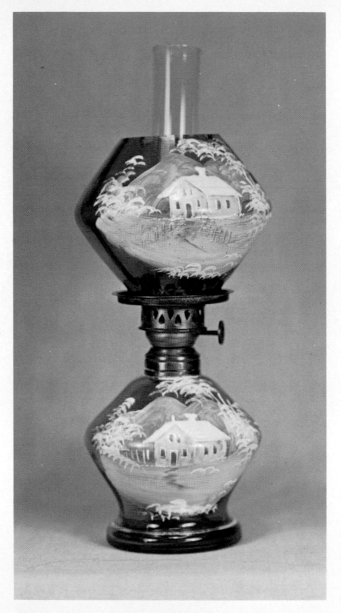

Fig. I. Green glass, enameled house and trees in white with gold bands; Nutmeg burner; 7½ inches high. Bates collection.

Miniature Lamps

by FRANK R. & RUTH E. SMITH

Schiffer Publishing Ltd

Box E, Exton, Pennsylvania 19341

Sixth printing, 1981

Copyright © 1968 by Frank R. and Ruth E. Smith

All rights reserved under International and Pan-American Conventions.
Published by special arrangement with Thomas Nelson, Inc., Publishers. Nashville,
Tennessee. Address inquiries to Schiffer Publishing Ltd., P. O. Box E, Exton, PA 19341

Designed by Harold Leach

ISBN 0-916838-44-7

Library of Congress Catalog Card Number: 68-57930

Printed in the United States of America

Acknowledgments

The authors take pleasure in thanking the many people who have helped in the preparation of this book. Mrs. Marcia Ray, Taneytown, Maryland; Mr. Albert Christian Revi, Hanover, Pennsylvania; and Mr. and Mrs. Brinton E. Sullivan, New Market, Maryland, loaned old catalogs and other papers containing illustrations and information on miniature lamps. To Mr. Revi special thanks are also due for reading the manuscript and for giving helpful advice and criticism throughout the progress of the work.

We are indebted to the Keystone View Company, Meadville, Pennsylvania, for permission to reproduce a stereoptican view card showing a miniature lamp.

We are grateful to the antique dealers who have notified us when they found miniature lamps and who imparted to us valuable information on lamps they had accumulated in their business.

The preparation of this book would not have been possible without the wholehearted cooperation of the collectors of miniature lamps. Not only were they willing to have the lamps in their collections photographed, but they entertained us royally when we visited them and gave us freely of their information on various lamps. We wish to sincerely thank these collectors: Mr. and Mrs. Carroll J. Agnew, Valley View Lane, Colonial Village, Wayne, Pennsylvania; Miss Kathalene Bankert, 122 York Street, Hanover, Pennsylvania; Mr. and Mrs. Fred C. Bartol, 425 South Buffalo Street, Warsaw, Indiana; Mr. and Mrs. Gerald M. Bates, 12 Foreside Road, Cumberland Foreside, Portland, Maine; Mr. and Mrs. Daniel C. Clark, 52444 Laurel Road, South Bend, Indiana; Mr. and Mrs. H. E. Funderwhite, Uwchland, Pennsylvania; Mr. and Mrs. James Lindemuth, 11 Linden Drive, Fair Haven, New Jersey; Mr. and Mrs. Paul Luckenbill, 407 Sunset Road, West Reading, Pennsylvania; Mr. and Mrs. Paul Myers, 1820 Lincoln Way, East, Lancaster, Pennsylvania; Mr. and Mrs. Harry Plasterer, 362 Sun Valley Road, Leola, Pennsylvania; Mr. and Mrs. C. H. Reinert, 287 Birch Lane, Hummelstown, Pennsylvania; Mr. and Mrs. Elmer L. Ritter, 2602 Market Street, Camp Hill, Pennsylvania; Mr. and Mrs. Ernest Rodney, Lincoln Way, East, Exton, Pennsylvania; Bob Schafer, 5355

Ivafern, La Canada, California; Sullivan's Antiques, 116 South Lime Street, Quarryville, Pennsylvania; Mr. and Mrs. Martin J. Wehle, 46 Stottle Road, Churchville, New York; Mr. and Mrs. Frederick W. Zies, 7617 Club Road, Ruxton, Maryland.

Contents

Foreword

In selecting lamps for the illustrations we have made every effort to include only those with proper matching shades. Because of this criterion several very attractive lamps were omitted. If we have made errors in selection or omission we ask the reader's forgiveness. This has been a difficult undertaking, for old catalogs showing miniature lamps are scarce and sometimes one shade seems to be as appropriate as another. Over the years broken shades have been replaced by others that in some cases seem to match. In some cases (Fig. 165, for example) the shades and bases show little resemblance in pattern but we are forced to conclude that they are original because they are so often found together. In other cases the base is frequently found with two different types of shades and illustrations in an old catalog show that both are proper (see Figs. 389 and 390). Still others came with either a matching ball shade or an umbrella shade (see Figs. 190 and 191). A few lamp bases without matching shades are included for study purposes.

When a lamp is found in more than one color or kind of glass we have listed all those we have seen; there may be others.

Some of the milk glass lamps can be found with different painted decorations. With such lamps we have made no attempt to photograph all of the various decorative patterns known.

The measurements given are to the top of the shade. These measurements may vary somewhat with different burners or because of the angle at which the arms of the tripod are bent. With lamps having no shade the measurements given are to the top of the brass collar.

We would like to have an index to enable the readers to readily locate the lamps in which they are most interested, but since very few of the lamp patterns have names such a listing is impractical.

We even found it difficult to arrange the illustrations in any logical order. The arrangement in which they are presented is not perfect but it is the best we could devise. If you are looking for a milk glass lamp and do not find it among these lamps it may be because this pattern was photographed in some other color. In that case you may have to thumb through the whole book. Again, we ask your indulgence.

Miniature Lamps

The Evolution of Lighting

Prehistoric Lighting

Fire as a means of illumination was doubtless appreciated by man as soon as its use was developed. The fire that warmed the crude shelters and caves of our ancestors also dispelled the gloom of the night, and a blazing stick would enable the more venturesome to penetrate deep into the dark recesses of a cave. For thousands of years, crude torches were the only portable light available. One of these hurled at a cave bear or a saber-toothed tiger may well have been primitive man's first effective weapon against these animals.

The first lamps of which we have record were used by primitive man to light his work as he carved or painted the walls of his cave. These were small hollowed-out stones in which animal fat was burned, probably with moss as a wick. One such lamp was found in the grotto of La Mouthe in France. The cave art in this grotto is considered to be early Magdalenian epoch of the Upper Palaeolithic period and the lamp is believed to be contemporary with it. The lamp is somewhat pear-shaped in outline and is ornamented with the engraved head and horns of an ibex. The artistic people who lived in and decorated the grotto were believed to be of the Cro-Magnon race and lived there some fifteen to twenty thousand years ago. From this humble beginning has evolved all of the oil- and fat-burning lamps that have appeared since that time. However, it is interesting to note that similar stone fat lamps were still in use among the peasants in the same region of France as late as 1915 and may still be used there today.

Our North American aborigines, with the exception of the Eskimo, apparently never used lamps of any kind. Even in their explorations of miles of underground caves they used only torches of wood, rushes, or similar materials. The Eskimo, however, used lamps of stone, clay, and bone, not only for light but for heat and cooking, using the fat of the seal, whale, or walrus for fuel.

Lamp Evolution in Historic Times

We will pass over very briefly the evolution of fat- and oil-lamp development from its beginning in the Stone Age until the second quarter of the nineteenth century. During this long period various animal fats and vegetable oils were used as fuel. In about A.D. 50, Pliny the Elder mentioned that mineral oil found along the shores of Asia was so used, being the first time this fuel was mentioned. The lamps themselves were changed in shape. The fuel reservoir was deepened from a slight depression and was covered over, leaving only a hole for filling and another spout-like opening for the wick. The material for the lamps was changed from stone to clay and eventually to bronze and other metals. These lamps were all small and, regardless of the material, remained much the same in general appearance and in operation. Judged by present-day standards of lighting, they would be considered practically worthless.

In 1490, Leonardo da Vinci enclosed the flame in a glass chimney fitted into a glass globe filled with water. Prior to this time the flame had been exposed. His invention reduced flickering and the chance of the flame being blown out by a gust of air. The light was also concentrated through the lens action of the water-filled globe, which seemed to have been the real reason for this development.

In 1784 Aimé Argand, a Swiss physicist, patented the lamp

which bears his name. The Argand lamp was really the first modern oil lamp and all oil lamps since then are largely patterned after it. It featured a round, hollow burner with a tubular wick and a glass chimney.

In the early nineteenth century, glass began to replace all other materials in lamp making. While some lamps were still made of metal and pottery, they were in the minority.

As has been pointed out, almost every combustible oil or fat—animal, vegetable, or mineral—was used in the small early lamps. Sometime prior to 1680, whale oil began to be used and continued as the favorite fuel until the scarcity of whales in the early nineteenth century made it prohibitive in price for most householders. People of modest means still used the small, fat lamps. In America the iron Betty lamp was the commonly used fat lamp.

In Boston, in 1821, sperm oil cost $1.07 per gallon on a contract basis, and this price continued to rise as whales became scarcer. The average householder was thus forced to depend on fat lamps or on candles for light and to use the whale oil lamp sparingly, if at all. In many cases the light of an open fire was considered quite satisfactory.

In 1830, Isaiah Jennings patented a new "burning fluid" consisting of eight parts of alcohol and one of turpentine. Others marketed mixtures of these substances as well as of camphor, rosin, and tincture of curcuma for use in lamps. In 1839, Augustus V. X. Webb put out a fluid consisting of distilled turpentine which he called "camphine." Later this name, spelled "camphene," has been applied to all of these "burning fluids."

The volatile nature of all of these fluids made them dangerous and many deaths and fires occurred as a result of their use. Attempts were made to improve or change the lamps to make them safer. It was felt that making longer wick tubes than those used for whale oil would help. Snuffers were also provided to extinguish the flame instead of blowing it out. These changes were not entirely satisfactory, but then a new fuel was developed which was to change the whole future of lighting devices throughout the world.

Torches and Candles Coexisted with Lamps

Man's earliest portable light was doubtless a flaming stick—a torch—and during all the development of lamps, the torches continued to be used. They were cheap and if made of wood, rushes, or other plant materials were nearly always readily available. If animal fats or similar substances were available to soak the torches, they gave even better light. Candles, really torches made of solid fats, were soon developed and used by the well-to-do. They were generally made of tallow or beeswax. Along coastal areas where wax myrtle or bayberry grew, the berries were gathered, the wax extracted, and fragrant greenish candles were made.

Metal torches, with a container at the top of the fuel, were also developed. However, some of the less affluent people continued to use sticks of lightwood into the nineteenth century.

Discovery and Use of Kerosene

About 1847, Samuel M. Kier of Pittsburgh began bottling the petroleum or rock oil from his father's salt wells near Tarentum, Pennsylvania, and selling it for medical purposes. In spite of his advertising circulars, which proclaimed it as "the most wonderful remedy ever discovered" for numerous ills, he soon found that he had a surplus of oil.

After consulting a Philadelphia chemist, Kier erected a one-barrel still on Seventh Avenue in Pittsburgh, about 1850. Here he distilled "carbon oil," or "kerosene" as it is now called, and sold it as an illuminant. Business boomed so that he soon installed a five-barrel still.

If the above date is correct, Kier apparently did not patent his process, for on March 27, 1855, Abraham Gesner of Williamsburg, New York, was granted a patent for making from petroleum or similar substances "a new liquid hydrocarbon, which I denominate 'kerosene.' " There were three grades of kerosene: A, B, and C. The heaviest, "C" grade, was suitable for lamps using a wick. This was apparently similar to what Kier had been making.

Since this lamp fuel was cheaper, safer, more nearly odorless, and gave a more brilliant light than fuels previously in use, it soon came into general use in western Pennsylvania and elsewhere. The demand soon exceeded the supply and the price rose from seventy-five cents to two dollars per gallon—a prohibitive price for those of moderate means.

The supply problem was finally solved on the afternoon of August 27, 1859, when oil was struck at the Drake well at Titusville, Pennsylvania. With a supply of crude oil assured, the use of this fuel for lighting spread rapidly and the development of the modern oil lamp was made possible.

The Passing of the Oil Lamp

Thomas A. Edison invented the first successful incandescent electric light bulb on October 21, 1879. Until 1905, these bulbs were rated on candle power, 16 being the most popular size. This size gave about twice as much light as a standard kerosene lamp or about as much as a 15-watt bulb today. Other bulbs gave 2, 4, and 8 candle power.

This invention marked the beginning of the end for the kerosene lamp, although the full effect of the invention was not felt for nearly a quarter of a century. As electricity became available in more homes, the oil lamps, in spite of their beauty and romantic charm, were thrown out or relegated to the attic where they gathered dust until rescued by the antique hunters of today. Even today many oil lamps are still in use where electricity is not available, or among people who because of their religion or some other reason prefer them.

Night or Miniature Lamps

Development of Miniature Lamps

Night or miniature oil lamps are replicas in miniature of the oil lamps that were in use before electric lights were available. By this we do not mean that every type or pattern of miniature lamp had a larger counterpart. While there is no hard and fast rule, perhaps a reasonable definition of a miniature or junior-sized lamp would be one that is too small to give adequate reading light for the period when it was made and used.

A lamp around twelve inches to the top of the shade is usually considered as miniature although many of them are much smaller. Above this size, smaller editions of large ornamental lamps are often referred to as junior-sized lamps. This includes the smaller copies of banquet lamps which are often called miniatures because they are so much smaller than their larger counterparts.

Glass miniature lamps appeared at an early date. Among the first items made at Sandwich were lamps, mentioned as early as July 30, 1825, less than a month after the factory opened. Some of these may well have been miniatures. They were sperm- or whale-oil lamps and were made to be used by burning the string-like wicks which were thrust through tubes in a cork. As various changes and improvements were made in lamps, miniature copies kept pace with the larger ones. As a matter of fact, many of the regularly used whale-oil lamps were so small as to be almost miniatures. Today small lamps with either the whale-oil or camphene type of burner are considered by most collectors as early lights and a collection to themselves.

In the 1850s, glass chimneys to enclose and protect the flame began to appear on lamps using kerosene. It is said that the lamp chimney was invented when a workman was heating a bottle over an open flame. The bottom of the bottle snapped off and the workman noticed how much brighter and more evenly the flame burned when the bottomless bottle was held over it. This may be the true origin of the modern lamp chimney. However, as we have seen, Leonardo da Vinci had used a chimney for protecting the flame centuries before.

Several different types of burners were soon developed to improve the burning and illuminating qualities of the lamps using the new fuel. The standard burner for miniature oil lamps was patented by L. J. Atwood on February 27, 1877. Shortly afterward, on March 20 and April 24, 1877, L. H. Olmsted patented another type of burner. The Olmsted burner is often called the Sandwich burner because it is often found in miniature Sandwich lamps. The development of these burners made possible the real beginning of minature lamps as they are known and collected today.

The first miniature oil lamps were simple and utilitarian in construction. Soon, however, a shade was added to enclose and protect the chimney and, in reality, to add beauty to the lamp. As the beautiful parlor lamps of the late Victorian age were developed, the miniature lamp also became more beautiful and elaborate. Almost every type of art glass known at the time appears in these lamps. It was indeed their golden age. It is these lamps that are so eagerly sought by collectors at the present time.

As oil lamps became obsolete some miniature electric lamps were made. Tiffany made some small electric lamps similar to those he made for candles and oil. In Europe some beautiful electric millefiore and cameo miniatures were produced, but judging by their scarcity, they were not numerous. Although much safer and more satisfactory than oil lamps, the miniature electric lamps never became popular in this country. In recent years some of the old oil miniatures have been converted for electricity.

In recent years the miniature oil lamp has staged a comeback in popularity. Many beautiful little lamps may now be found in both glass and porcelain in art and gift shops. Many of these are imports, but some are of domestic manufacture. It is to be regretted that some antique dealers handle these and, through ignorance or greed, offer them as old at fantastic prices. Recently such a dealer offered one to us for $135.00. At a nearby gift shop similar lamps were available for $7.50.

The Use of Miniature Lamps

Miniature lamps were used for a number of purposes, but some dealers and collectors champion one or another of these uses to the exclusion of all the others. In most old catalogs they are referred to as "night lamps," which really tells little as to

9477—Undergoing Repairs.

A stereopticon card of 1899 showing a "Sylvan" miniature lamp; put out by Keystone View Company, Meadville, Pa. We wish to thank the company for permission to reproduce this picture. See also Fig. 296.

21

their use but leaves the buyer to use his purchase as he sees fit.

As night lights they were doubtless often used as a dim light to burn through the night after the big lamps had been extinguished. They would also make good lights for sick rooms, for the elderly, or for children's rooms.

We have a stereoptican card (see page 21), with the copyright date of 1899, showing two little girls in their bedroom preparing to retire. On a table by the bed is a miniature lamp like that shown in Fig. 296. Doubtless a child would feel safe and secure with the soft light of such a lamp to frighten away bogey men and other such "dangers" that might creep up in the dark.

Doubtless many of the little lamps were given to children for their rooms or playhouses. I, myself, had two of the little lamps in my playhouse, and years later these two were the foundation on which our collection was based. Somewhere we have seen an advertisement of a special oil can showing a mother filling a large parlor lamp while by her side stands a little girl holding her miniature lamp to be filled.

The Time and Light (Fig. 23) could be placed by the bed, and if the sleeper awakened during the night the oil level in the lamp would tell the time. One of our friends tested the lamp and found that it was surprisingly accurate when equipped with the original burner and string-like wick. Some of these lamps are now found equipped with nutmeg burners with the flat wicks. Such lamps have lost their utility as timepieces.

Some people claim that these time lamps were courting lamps, lighted when the beau arrived at eight in the evening, and used to time his visit. Perhaps this is true, but since the lamp tells time for ten hours (from eight until six) it seems more probable that it was a night lamp. In those days, early to bed and early to rise was the rule, while a suitor who lingered until six in the morning would certainly have been frowned upon by any strict parent.

Some claim that all miniatures were courting lamps to be used in the parlor when the young lady of the house had a caller. Doubtless one of these beautiful lamps would add an aura of

22

charm and romance, while the dim light would answer all the requirements of propriety for lovers.

The miniatures may also have served as salesmen's samples to show the prospective purchasers what the standard-sized lamps were like. We have had antique dealers tell us that the original owners, from whom they purchased the lamp, said that it was a drummer's sample given to them or some of their relatives. Comparatively few of the miniature lamps, however, have larger counterparts, so this premise seems unfounded. Possibly such lamps were given to retailers who gave the drummer a substantial order. In at least one case (Fig. 270), a clothier in Washington, Pennsylvania, gave these little lamps to his customers, possibly in place of calendars at Christmas.

Lastly, since many of the lamps were beautifully made of the finest and most colorful glass, they were ornaments in their own right. At the time of their manufacture, the late Victorian and Gay 90s period, they would have fitted right into the elaborately decorated surroundings. Many of the most beautiful examples show little if any signs of use so that some were probably bought and used only as ornaments.

The Component Parts of a Miniature Lamp

Even the most simply constructed miniature lamp is composed of several separate parts. From a study of these parts it is sometimes possible to determine the age of the lamp, the country of origin, and also if the lamp is all original.

The collector must not loose sight of the fact that over the years burners may have been changed or that chimneys have been broken and replaced. He must remember that there is little information on just how most lamps were originally equipped. A Nutmeg lamp, which was made in America, with a foreign burner has obviously been tampered with, but in many cases the collector will have to rely on his own experience and judgment in forming his opinion. We will give a few observations on the various parts of the lamps in the hopes that they will be found interesting and helpful.

23

The Base. The base or oil font with the attached collar is often all that remains of a lamp. Many bases so found are then provided with burners and chimneys and some people assure the customer that the lamp is complete. In the case of many hand lamps and stem lamps this is true, but with most fancy bases the collector should be skeptical. It must not be forgotten that it is very difficult to find a matching shade for such a base and an incomplete lamp is of limited value to a serious collector.

Collars. Collars are the metal caps, usually of brass, on top of the font into which the burners are screwed. The most common type on both the miniature and standard-sized lamps fits loosely over an elevated lip molded on top of the font. They were originally attached with plaster of Paris, but some are now found fastened on with putty. This appears to be the collar patented by George W. Brown of Forestville, Connecticut, on March 21, 1876, although some are marked "Pat'd Apr. 13, 1876 & Mch. 21, 1878." This type of miniature collar is about an inch in diameter, and takes either an Acorn or a Nutmeg burner. Most have nearly straight sides but others have sloping sides or flare out at the bottom. Some are very plain, others are variously ornamented with rings or knurls. Some, that appear to be of late manufacture, screw onto threads molded on the top of the glass font. We have never noticed patent dates or manufacturers' names on any of these late collars.

Another type of collar that also takes the Nutmeg and Acorn burners appears to be rather rare. It consists of a narrow band of brass (⅞ of an inch in diameter) embedded in the glass at the top of the font. In the glass around some of these is embossed in very small and indistinct letters "Patented Sept. 19 & Nov. 14, 1911." Some have no such markings. We have never seen this collar in any except the small size.

Collars for the Hornet-sized burners are made in the same way as the smaller sizes. They are about one and a half inches in diameter. Collars for standard-sized lamps are but larger editions of those for small lamps.

Collars attached with plaster of Paris were apparently rarely replaced on lamps. If the plaster of Paris gave way, the collar was reattached rather than being replaced by a new one.

A third type of collar is also about one and a half inches in diameter, and is screwed onto the threaded top of the glass font instead of being permanently attached with plaster of Paris. This type takes the Nutmeg and Acorn burners. Some of these screw-top bases were also equipped with perforated tops and put out in pairs as salt and pepper shakers. That they were also originally put out as lamps is proved by the fact that some types have matching globe-chimney shades. Others have only the burner and chimney and apparently never had a matching shade.

Somewhat similar lamps with a two-inch screw-on collar are also found. They take either the Nutmeg and Acorn or the Hornet burner. These collars are often of tin rather than of brass, and the lamps are pressed glass and rather cheap looking. They have matching globe or umbrella shades or, in the case of the Hornet burner, a globe-chimney shade. We have never seen these bases equipped with shaker tops.

There are several other collars that differ somewhat from those described but it does not seem worthwhile to give details for all of them. Foreign collars are generally very similar to those made in America. The screw-on type of collar seems to be rare in foreign lamps except on those of very recent manufacture.

Burners. Five types of burners of American manufacture are found on miniature lamps. The three most commonly found, the Nutmeg, the Acorn, and the Hornet, were all made by the Plume and Atwood Manufacturing Company of Waterbury, Connecticut, under Patent #187,800, which was issued February 27, 1877, to L. J. Atwood, and assigned to the company. This company also made the Victor burner for junior-sized lamps. This burner resembles European burners for the same type of lamps. They also made burners similar to the Olmsted for very small lamps. These burners seem to have had no specific name on them, at least we have found none marked. It may be

The three most common burners in miniature lamps are *(left to right)* the Acorn, the Hornet, and the Nutmeg. This illustration is from a catalog of the Plume and Atwood Manufacturing Company.

that unmarked burners, or those marked only by stars or other ornaments, were made by other companies.

Nutmeg burners are variously marked on the wheel of the wick raiser. What appears to be older ones are marked "Pat. Feb'y 27, 1877." Others, probably of later manufacture, are marked "P & A Mfg. Co.," "Made in U.S.A." or ornamented with a twelve-pointed star design. A silver burner on a lamp ornamented with silver filigree is marked "E. M. & Co."

Recently-made burners are marked "The P. & A. Mfg. Co. Acorn"; they resemble the old Nutmeg burners in shape.

The Acorn burners are also variously marked. What appears to be older ones are marked "The P. & A. Mfg. Co. Acorn." Others are ornamented with a circle of six dots, while others are plain with no marks or ornaments whatsoever.

Both the Nutmeg and Acorn burners take either a ring for the ball and upturned shades, or a tripod for umbrella shades. These fixtures come separately but slip down over the ring of prongs which holds the chimney. In older burners a distinct ring-like ledge held the fixtue neatly and securely in place. In late burners this ring is not so well formed.

Both the Nutmeg and the Acorn burners take a chimney a little over an inch in diameter.

The Hornet burner resembles the Acorn in general appearance but is larger; it takes a chimney one and a half inches in diameter. These burners also take a ring for ball shades or a tripod for umbrella shades. Umbrella shades are rare with the Hornet-sized burners. By far the greater number of lamps equipped with Hornet-sized burners have globe-chimney shades.

Hornet burners may be marked "P. & A. Hornet" or are plain with no marks or ornaments. One of this size was marked "Crown Improved" and was probably not made by the Plume and Atwood Company.

A foreign burner is somewhat similar to the Acorn in size and shape but is smaller, taking a chimney fifteen sixteenths of an inch in diameter. Since it is of European make it probably could properly be referred to as two and a half centimeters in size. The greater number of these are marked "Spar-Brenner," but others are marked "T & B Rukle," "Wienerbrenner Prima," "Korner & Co. Berlin," or have a pattern of diamonds and dots. The ring holder for the ball or upturned shade is usually securely attached to the upper part of the burner.

Another type of foreign burner takes a chimney one and an eighth to one and a quarter inches in diameter. Often these are the student-lamp type of chimney. It takes a globe type of shade and was probably made in Germany, for one of these lamps has "Gute Nacht" on the globe. The wick raisers are variously ornamented but we have seen none with names, legends, or dates.

The junior-sized lamps usually have burners taking a chimney one and a half inches in diameter. Many of the chimneys are of the student-lamp type. These burners take a flat wick which, because of the construction of the burner, emerges through the top in the shape of a circle or ring. With foreign burners of this type the wick is inserted through a crescent-shaped opening in the bottom. With American burners the opening for inserting the wick is ⊏ shaped. We have seen one such burner equipped with two narrow wicks instead of one wider one, probably because a wide wick was not available.

The American burners are marked "The P & A M'F'G Co Victor" and "J. Dardonville, N.Y."

Foreign burners of this type are variously marked:

"Prima—Rund—Brenner"
"Super—Rund—Brenner"
"Kosmos"
"R. R. F. Paris"
An "H" surrounded by rays forming an eight-pointed
     star-like pattern
A circle of stars and rays
Other complicated ornaments

The fifth type of American burner is very small and entirely different in shape from the others. It takes a tiny string wick. Some collectors call it the Sandwich burner because this is the type found on the Sandwich lamps. It was patented by Leverett H. Olmsted of Brooklyn, N.Y., on March 20, and April 24, 1877. These burners take no chimney, the shade serving as both shade and chimney. There are several variants of this burner. A few are marked "P. & A. Mfg. Co.," but most are unmarked and it is not known who made them. One variant is found on the Vapo-Cresolene vaporizer.

Some dealers and collectors persist in dating a lamp from the patent date on the wick raiser of the burner if such a date is present. This is a fallacy since such hardware was manufactured for many years after the patent was issued. Furthermore, burners were often replaced so that there is no way of telling if it is original equipment.

The amount of tarnish on a burner is a poor way to judge age unless you have had considerable experience. We have known unscrupulous people to place new burners and other lamp hardware in a chemical to tarnish them. The lamps were then sold as old.

Chimneys. Chimneys for the Nutmeg- and Acorn-sized burners come in various lengths from three and a quarter to five inches. Since chimneys are often replaced or are absent on lamps as found, some collectors either leave them off or supply

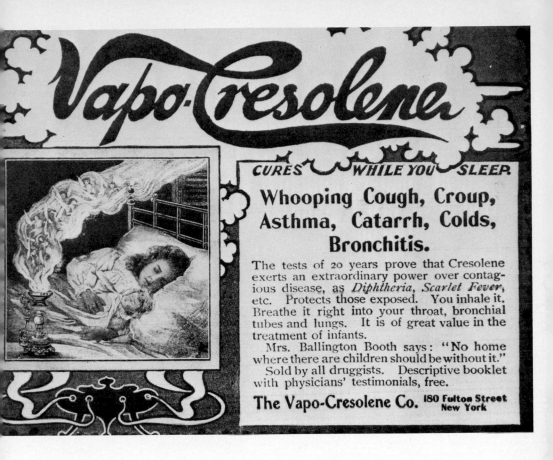

An advertisement from an old magazine showing the Vapo-Cresolene vaporizing lamp in operation. See Fig. 630.

their lamps with a chimney length that looks best. Apparently most original chimneys were made of clear glass but a few years ago reproduction chimneys in several colors made their appearance. Some frosted miniature chimneys also appeared about the same time. The cranberry Mary Gregory-type lamp had a tall cranberry chimney when found and it appears to be original. A few other lamps also have matching chimneys.

Several years ago Bob Shafer located an original box of old chimneys of an unusual type. They were for the Nutmeg-Acorn burners, three and a half inches tall with pleatings extending one and a half inches down the sides from the top (Fig. 47). He generously shared some of these chimneys with us.

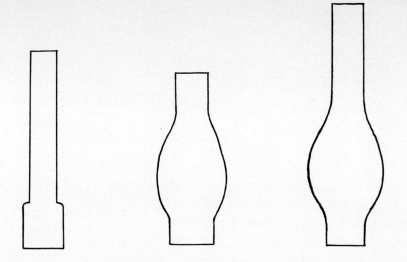

Three types of miniature lamp chimneys. *Left:* Student-lamp chimney. Some foreign lamps have this type of chimney. *Center and right:* Short and long chimneys of the type usually found on American lamps. Many foreign lamps use chimneys similar to the long type, but they are slightly smaller in diameter.

Most foreign burners require a fifteen-sixteenth-inch chimney that is about five and a half inches tall. These foreign lamps quite often lack chimneys and it is hard to locate replacements for them.

Chimneys for the Hornet burners also came in various lengths. Often lamps requiring the Hornet burners come with chimney-shades requiring no clear chimneys.

Some foreign lamps are equipped with the student-lamp type chimney. The smaller chimneys of this type fit on burners using a round string-like wick. Many foreign lamps of the junior size use student-lamp type chimneys. These lamps are equipped with burners using flat wicks but are so constructed that the wick is rolled into a ring as it emerges from the burner.

Shades. An oil reservoir equipped with a suitable burner, wick, and chimney constitute a usable light-giving lamp. The simplest miniature lamps are nothing more. The more ornate examples were made with some type of shade to hide the flame, diffuse the light, and add beauty to the lamp. There are four general types of shades: the globe or ball shade; the umbrella, mushroom, or half shade; the upturned or inverted shade; and the globe-chimney shade.

The globe shade is more or less round in shape and rests on a ring or platform attached to the burner. It requires a chimney to enclose and protect the flame.

The umbrella, also called mushroom or half shade, usually rests on a tripod attached to the burner. Sometimes a metal ring-like holder is attached to the ends of the tripod arms and in this the shade rests. In some instances the burner is equipped with two metal strips which pass up on each side of the chimney and support a metal ring about the top of the chimney. On this ring the shade hangs supported by its narrow top. In a few cases shades supported in this manner are made of cloth or wicker work instead of glass. A chimney to protect the flame is used with all umbrella shades.

The upturned or inverted shade rests on a ring about the burner like that used for the globe shade. The shade flares out toward the top like an opened tulip or a bowl. The top edge of the shade may be ornamented with ruffles or an applied glass rim in contrasting color. Many of the more ornate and beautiful lamps have upturned shades. A chimney is used with these shades.

Types of shades for miniature lamps. *Left to right:* Umbrella, Half-shade, or Mushroom type; Ball type; Globe-chimney type; and Upturned or Inverted type.

The globe-chimney shade fits inside the top of the burner in place of a separate glass chimney. Just above the burner it flares out giving room for the flame of the lamp. At the top it is constricted to form a chimney-like opening. A separate chimney is never used with this type of shade. Many of these shades are ornamented with embossed flowers or designs which causes great variation in the thickness of the glass. Since this variation in glass thickness would cause uneven distribution of the heat of the flame, this may be the reason so many of these shades are found cracked.

In colored lamps it sometimes happens that while the pattern of the base and shade match there is a slight difference in the color of the two parts. This can be explained by the two parts being made from different batches of glass. In some cases a difference in the thickness of the glass will also influence the color of the finished piece. It is probable that first-quality lamps had perfectly matching bases and shades when originally sold and discriminating collectors prefer these perfectly matched lamps today.

In painted lamps the paint, unless well fired on, is likely to be partly worn or washed off. This is particularly true of gilt which is sometimes almost entirely gone.

Some clear-glass lamps were painted to resemble either red satin or milk glass. This paint is very easily removed and such lamps are often found without a trace of paint either because it has all been removed or they had never been painted at all. The clear-glass cosmus lamp is one such example.

Other Miniature Lamps of the Kerosene Period

There are two other types of lamp coexisting with the miniature oil lamps which we will mention briefly. Both are interesting and in one group is found some of the most beautiful glass creations ever made.

Fig. II. Left: Milk glass in a swirl pattern with flowers in intaglio design (Impressed below the surface); fired-on orange paint around top of shade and base; red, orange, and green; Hornet burner; 8¾ inches high. Authors' collection. Center: Yellow satin glass, fired-on pink, brown, and green flowers and leaves; Nutmeg burner; 7¼ inches high; made by Consolidated Lamp and Glass Co., Pittsburgh, Pa., about 1894. Wehle collection. Right: Brass pedestal base; milk glass lamp; shade and font with painted green trim, ornamented with red roses and green leaves. Nutmeg burner; 9¾ inches high. Found also in blue milk glass painted pink shading to white with yellow and red pansies. Authors' collection.

Fig. III. Artichoke lamps; Nutmeg burners; 8 inches high. In addition to colors shown here, artichoke lamps are found in green opalescent.

Fig. IV. White metal spray of leaves and buds; pink cased glass with rows of applied clear glass shells around base, shade, and candle-holders; foreign burner; 9½ inches high. Authors' collection.

Glow Lamps. This type of miniature lamp burned oil but is very different in construction from the common oil lamps (see Figs. 624 though 628). The base is wide and flat and usually both base and shade are ribbed. Some shades have molded notches inside the bottom which fit into slots in the base so that a quarter turn makes them secure. Others have a metal collar into which the top or shade fits.

The burner consists of a glass tube with an expanded pear-shaped bulb at the top. Into this the string-type wick fits enclosed in a spiral twisted wire which acts as a wick raiser. As the expanded bulb on the glass tube is very thin and fragile, it is often broken and the lamp is found without the glass tube and spiral wire.

There are several patterns of these lamps, all much alike. They also come in several colors: clear, red, amber, blue, green, and milk glass. Sometimes the top and bottom do not match either in color or pattern but these specimens are probably made up of the remains of two lamps. Some of the milk glass lamps are decorated with nicely painted flowers.

Fairy Lamps. The Fairy lamps were another type of small, night lamp which burned candles (Fig. 629). They were introduced by Clark's Pyramid and Fairy Light Company of London, England, beginning about 1844.

They consisted of a variously shaped and ornamented base, a small cup for the candle, and a dome-shaped shade. The shade was often very beautifully made of the finest glass and often splendidly ornamented. Some of the shades were in the shape of castles, animals' or birds' heads, or other fantastic shapes. Some of these lamps were used singly, others in beautiful and artistic clusters. Certain types are still made and sold.

Miniature Lamps

Fig. 1. Early whale-oil lamp; cobalt blue base; clear font; tin-cork drop-in burner; 5 inches high. *Zies collection.*

Fig. 2. Clear pattern-glass whale-oil lamp; double pewter wick holder; 7¾ inches high. *Authors' collection.*

Fig. 3. Clear glass lamp with applied handle; camphene type pewter wick holder and snuffer; 5¾ inches high. *Authors' collection.*

37

Fig. 4. Pale green glass with tin burner and reflector; embossed in glass is "The London Lamp"; 5¾ inches to top of reflector. *Authors' collection.*

Fig. 5. Two types of "Handy lamps." *Left:* Green glass; embossed name "Handy" on base; clear chimney; Acorn burner; 3¾ inches high. *Right:* Clear glass; embossed name "T. E. Handy—M" on base; tin burner and reflector; 6¼ inches to top of reflector. *Both in Reinert collection.*

Fig. 6. Clear glass with applied handle; embossed name "Fire-Fly" and stars; string-type burner; 2½ inches high. *Bates collection.*

38

Fig. 7. Two "Little Fire-Fly" lamps, one with handle; embossed with stars and a design; white shades; Olmsted burners; 4½ inches high. *Agnew collection.*

Fig. 8. Brass chandelier; clear glass fonts with milk glass shades; fonts marked "Fire-Fly"; 10½ inches high. *Schafer collection.*

39

Fig. 14. "Little Harry's" bracket lamp; cast-iron bracket gilted gold, embossed "Little Harry's Night Lamp"; clear glass font embossed on side "L. H. Olmsted. New York," on bottom "Pat. Mar. 20 Apr. 24, 1877"; string wick; clear glass chimney-shade embossed "Little Harry's Night Lamp"; 6 inches high. *Agnew collection.*

Fig. 15. Clear glass base; milk glass chimney; embossed in base "Little Harry's Night Lamp. L. H. Olmsted, New York"; 3½ inches high. *Bartol collection.*

Fig. 16. *Left:* Clear glass, embossed name "Little Favorite" on roughened band around center; applied handle; Nutmeg burner; 2½ inches high. *Right:* Clear glass, embossed name "Little Beauty" on smooth band around center; applied handle; Nutmeg burner; 2½ inches high. (Two other lamps, "Little Pearl" and "Little Wide Awake" are very similar.) *Both in Reinert collection.*

Fig. 17. Milk glass with embossed name "Little Harry's Night Lamp" on font and embossed stars on base; milk glass shade; Olmsted burner; 6½ inches high. *Reinert collection.*

Fig. 18. Silver base, cranberry glass font with enameled flower sprays in white and yellow; white opalescent chimney; burner marked "P. & A."; string wick; 6 inches high. *Agnew collection.*

43

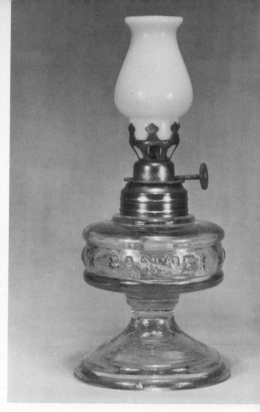

Fig. 19. Clear glass ribbed pattern with embossed name "Little Twilight" on base; white Bristol shade; Olmsted burner; 7 inches high. *Reinert collection.*

Fig. 20. "Improved Banner" lamp; clear glass with embossed "Improved Banner" and three stars on base; white Bristol shade; Olmsted-type burner made by P. & A. Co.; 3 inches high. Found also in milk glass. *Authors' collection.*

Fig. 21. Clear glass embossed design; white Bristol shade; Olmsted-type burner; 5 inches high. Found also painted red, paint not fired-on. *Authors' collection.*

Fig. 22. (on facing page) Clear glass with embossed ribs and plumes; name "Noxall" on bottom; white Bristol shade; unmarked burner; 6¼ inches high. *Authors' collection.*

Fig. 23. Time Lamp; clear glass, embossed "Time & Light. Pride of America. Grand Vals Perfect Time Indicating Lamp" and time marks from 8 to 6; white embossed Shell pattern shade; unmarked burner; 6¾ inches high. Also found with white bee-hive type shade. Pictured in Butler Brothers' catalog "Our Drummer" for Feb. 1900 with a caption reading: "This lamp is a decided novelty. The time is indicated on the graduated scale, and is adjusted to the consumption of oil with nearly the precision of a clock. As a night lamp it is superior to any lamp ever made for that purpose, there being positively no odor emitted while burning." Price $4.50 per dozen. *Authors' collection.*

Fig. 24. Milk glass with embossed Shell design; decorated in gold gilt which is badly worn; string-type burner; 4¾ inches high. *Authors' collection.*

Fig. 25. Bristol white, decorated with gold bands and a blue and green floral band; Olmsted-type burner; 4½ inches high. *Lindemuth collection.*

Fig. 26. Blue Bristol glass, enameled flowers in orange, blue, and green with narrow red bands; white Bristol shade; foreign burner; 6½ inches high. *Authors' collection.*

Fig. 27. Gilded white metal; white Bristol shade; round string-type wick; 4½ inches high. Said to be German, ca. 1880-1890. *Lindemuth collection.*

46

Fig. 28. Blue opaline base, white opaline shade, both with embossed designs; Olmsted-type burners; 5½ inches high. Found also in green opalescent. *Authors' collection.*

Fig. 29. Clear glass "Nutmeg" lamp; embossed "Nutmeg" on font; narrow brass band forms removable handle; Nutmeg burner; 2¾ inches high. Found also in milk glass, green, and cobalt blue. Pictured in C. M. Linnington's catalog "Silent Salesman" for Jan. 1894 at $1.41 per dozen. *Authors' collection.*

Fig. 30. Green glass lamp set in tin holder; embossed in glass "Manila. Pat. Appl'd For"; Acorn burner; 2¾ inches high. Found also in milk glass and in crystal. *Authors' collection.*

47

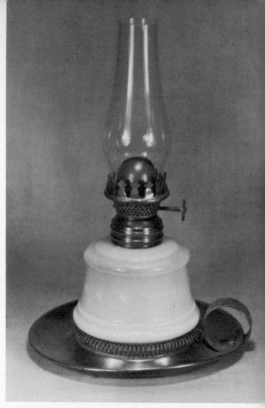

Fig. 31. Brass saucer lamp; Nutmeg burner; 2 inches high. *Authors' collection.*

Fig. 32. "Little Duchess" lamp; opalescent milk glass with embossed "Little Duchess" and three stars; brass saucer base and brass spring to hold lamp securely; Acorn burner; 3 inches high. Found also in blue glass. *Authors' collection.*

Fig. 33. Green glass lamp attached to a square tin saucer; Acorn burner; 2½ inches high. Also found in blue glass. Pictured in Butler Brothers' catalog "Our Drummer" for Apr. 1912 at 85¢ per dozen. *Authors' collection.*

48

Fig. V. Left to right: Rainbow glossy finish mother-of-pearl in Raindrop pattern; row of applied clear glass shells around top and bottom of base; foreign burner; 9¾ inches high. Found also in blue. Silver pedestal base; rainbow mother-of-pearl satin finish in Diamond pattern; foreign burner; 10½ inches high. Rainbow mother-of-pearl satin finish in Diamond pattern; applied frosted feet; foreign burner; 9¾ inches high. Found also in blue. Authors' collection.

Fig. VI. Bisque, brown face with brown glass eyes; dressed in black, yellow, and blue; foreign burner; 6½ inches high. Schafer collection.

Fig. VII. Santa Claus lamp; milk glass; base is white mound of snow and black boots; shade is the body, clothing reddish-orange, whiskers marked with gray; Nutmeg burner; 9½ inches high. Made by Consolidated Lamp and Glass Co., Pittsburgh, Pa., about 1894. Authors' collection.

Fig. VIII. Cameo lamp; white maidenhair fern and butterflies on citron ground; marked "RD 63474" (Stevens and Williams); foreign burner; 7¾ inches high. Wehle collection.

Fig. IX. Left: Diamond pattern, mother-of-pearl satin glass, dark shading to very light pink with enameled blue and white flowers; Nutmeg burner; 7 inches high. Right: Candy-stripe pink and white cased glass with white lining; applied clear glass shell feet; Nutmeg burner; 8½ inches high. Authors' collection.

Fig. X. Left: Milk glass painted dark green about top of base and shade and with large pink roses; Nutmeg burner; 8¾ inches high. Found also with other floral designs. Right: Standing Elephant lamp; porcelain base in dark ivory color trimmed in brown and gold; milk glass shade with fired-on matching colors; Nutmeg burner; 9¾ inches high. Authors' collection.

Fig. XI. Cranberry glass, amber applied berries; foreign burner; 8 inches high. Bates collection.

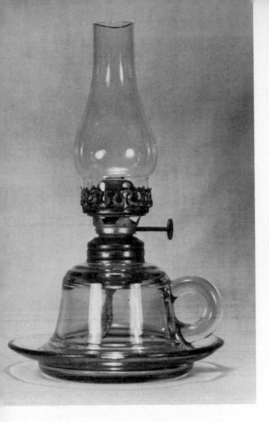

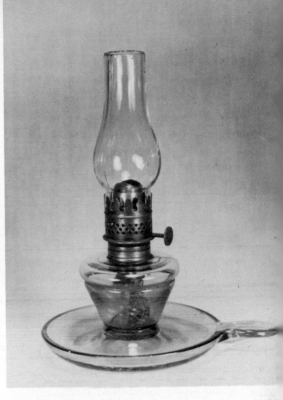

Fig. 34. Upside-down cup and saucer lamp; light amber glass; Hornet-type burner with name "Sterling"; 3½ inches high. *Agnew collection.*

Fig. 35. Amber glass; Nutmeg burner; 9 inches high. *Bartol collection.*

Fig. 36. "Little Buttercup" lamp; blue glass with applied handle and embossed name "Little Buttercup"; Nutmeg burner; 2¾ inches high. Found also in crystal, amber, amethyst, and frosted clear glass. *Authors' collection.*

49

Fig. 37. Clear glass with embossed elephant, two moons, and two stars; applied handle; Acorn burner; 2¾ inches high. *Authors' collection.*

Fig. 38. Spatter glass, white with various shades of blue and pink; applied handle; Nutmeg burner; 3 inches high. *Authors' collection.*

Fig. 39. Milk glass decorated with blue and red paint; red berries and green and gray leaves; painted blue band around top of lamp; red lines around top and bottom; Nutmeg burner; 3 inches high. Found also with other painted decorations. *Authors' collection.*

Fig. 40. Blue, with square Spanish lace design in white and blue applied handle; Hornet burner; 3 inches high. *Agnew collection.*

Fig. 41. Crystal glass, embossed design; Nutmeg burner; 2 inches high. *Zies collection.*

Fig. 42. Clear glass, embossed sun with rays and plant; applied clear handle; Hornet burner; 2½ inches high. *Reinert collection.*

Fig. 49. Paneled blue glass; applied handle; foreign burner; 6½ inches high. *Bartol collection.*

Fig. 50. Log Cabin or Schoolhouse lamp; amber glass, embossed; applied handle; Hornet burner; 3¾ inches high. Found also in clear, blue, white opaline, and milk glass. Sometimes found with a No. 2 burner. *Authors' collection.*

Fig. 51. Clear glass Shoe lamp; applied handle pressed into place; Hornet burner; 3½ inches high. Found also in blue and amber glass. Made by Atterbury & Co. of Pittsburgh, Pa., ca. 1860. *Authors' collection.*

54

Fig. 52. Match-holder lamp; amber glass with embossed ribs; match-holder is in basket-weave pattern; Nutmeg burner; 8 inches high. Found also in crystal, blue, and milk glass. Also found with Hornet burner and larger shade to fit. *Authors' collection.*

Fig. 53. Milk glass, embossed design; Acorn burner; 3 inches high. This lamp fastened to a brass saucer base was called "Virginia" in the 1896-97 catalog of Dodd, Werner & Co. of Cincinnati, Ohio, and sold for $4.00 per dozen. *Clark collection.*

Fig. 54. Embossed milk glass with brass band; iron ring for handle; Nutmeg burner; 3 inches high. In the Dodd, Werner & Co. (Cincinnati, Ohio) trade catalog for 1896-97, this lamp was called "Brownie." See Fig. 56. *Authors' collection.*

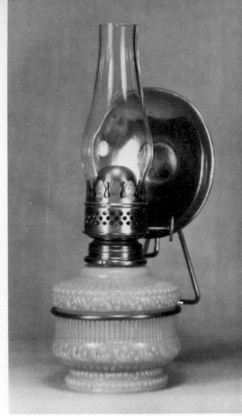

Fig. 55. *Left:* Clear glass with embossed design and attached reflector; Nutmeg burner; 7¼ inches high. *Right:* Same base, painted a dull blue to look satin, and decorated in gold; clear glass chimney in matching embossed design. Also found in white opalescent. *Both in Authors' collection.*

Fig. 56. Embossed blue milk glass with brass hanger and nickel reflector; Nutmeg burner; 3 inches high to top of collar. Found also in white milk glass. In Butler Brothers' catalog "Our Drummer" for Feb. 1900 this lamp was illustrated and called "Katy Did"; priced at $4.00 per dozen. See Fig. 54. *Authors' collection.*

Fig. 57. Blue milk glass with embossed design and nickel reflector; Acorn burner; 2½ inches high. *Clark collection.*

56

Fig. 58. Cobalt blue with metal hanger and mirror reflector; foreign burner; 2¼ inches high. *Authors' collection.*

Fig. 59. Brass lamp with nickel reflector; Hornet burner; 2¾ inches high. *Authors' collection.*

Fig. 60. Tin hanging lamp with reflector and Bristol shade; British burner; 2½ inches to top of base. *Authors' collection.*

57

Fig. 62. Lockwood Concentrated Light; polished nickel; Nutmeg burner; 8 inches high. Found in old store in original crumbling box with directions to attach to desk, workbench, or sewing machine. Pat. Apr. 3, 1883. See also Fig. 63. *Authors' collection.*

Fig. 61. Tin hanging lamp with reflector; painted red; Nutmeg burner; 5¼ inches to top of reflector. *Authors' collection.*

Fig. 63. Label from the crumbling pasteboard box in which the Lockwood lamp was found. See Fig. 62.

Fig. 64. "Acme" nickel-plated night lamp with reflector; Hornet burner; 4 inches to top of burner. "Made in U.S.A. by Edward Miller & Co." *Plasterer collection.*

Fig. 65. Brass lamp with nickel reflector; Nutmeg burner; 7½ inches to top of reflector. *Authors' collection.*

Fig. 66. White metal base; Tiffany-type shade in clear glass, frosted on inside; Hornet burner; 7½ inches high. *Zies collection.*

59

Fig. 67. Brass plated lamp; Hornet burner; 3¾ inches high. *Authors' collection.*

Fig. 68. Pewter lamp; burner marked "Stellar. E. M. & Co" (Edward Miller & Co.); 3½ inches high. *Agnew collection.*

Fig. 69. Brass boudoir lamp with embroidered batiste and lace shade; Nutmeg burner; 7 inches high. *Authors' collection.*

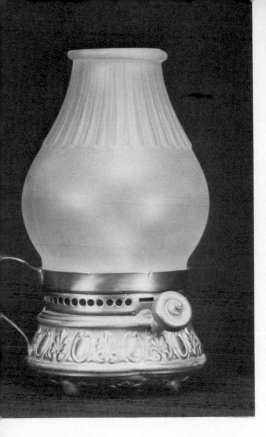

Fig. 70. Brass lamp; frosted glass shade; wick-tube inserted at an angle and wick-raiser operates at an angle; 6 inches high. *Zies collection.*

Fig. 72. Aladdin-type lamp in nickel; Bristol shade; unmarked burner; 3½ inches to top of handle. *Authors' collection.*

Fig. 71. Pottery painted orange, paint partly worn off; embossed Cupid on one side, horns and arrows on the other; screw-on collar; foreign burner; 2¾ inches high. *Bartol collection.*

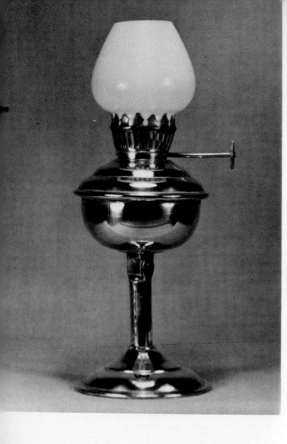

Fig. 73. Brass pedestal lamp with hinged stem; white Bristol shade; stem of lamp can be bent so base can be attached to wall; foreign burner; 7½ inches high. See Fig. 74. *Authors' collection.*

Fig. 74. Brass pedestal lamp with hinged stem bent in position for attaching to wall. See Fig. 73.

Fig. 75. Crystal Aladdin lamp, said to be Sandwich; Hornet burner; 3½ inches high. *Schafer collection.*

62

Fig. 76. Brass pedestal lamp with swinging font; white Bristol shade; font swings so base of pedestal can be attached to wall; foreign burner; 8½ inches high. *Bartol collection.*

Fig. 77. Brass "Beauty Night Lamp"; oil is poured in through opening at top of bracket; lion's mouth holds tubing; said to burn 40 hours; most of these lamps are nickel plated; milk glass shade; 4½ inches high. *Authors' collection.*

Fig. 78. Nickel lamp; embossed name "Comet"; blue bee-hive shade; 7¼ inches to top of burner. These are often called "Beauty Lamps" and were said to have been used on either side of a dresser. *Lindemuth collection.*

Fig. 79. Brass Barrel lamp; frosted glass shade with painted decorations in red and white; foreign burner; 7 inches to top of shade. *Wehle collection.*

Fig. 80. Brass Fire Engine lamp; Acorn burner; 5½ inches high. *Wehle collection.*

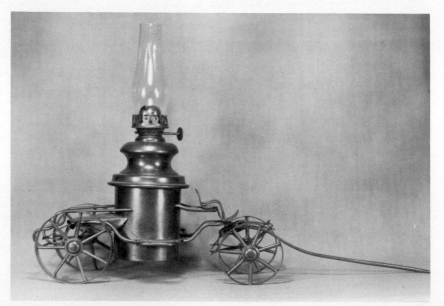

Fig. 81. Double-burner log pig-type brass lamp with pan over one side for spices for scenting room; "Patented Oct. 28—79"; Nutmeg burner; 2½ inches to top of collar; 7 inches to top of spice holder. *Wehle collection.*

Fig. 82. Brass Sleigh lamp; "Oct. 28 79" on base; milk glass shade; Nutmeg burner; 6 inches high. *Rodney collection.*

Fig. 83. Student lamp; brass with white Bristol shade; Olmsted burner; 7¾ inches to top of ring; said to have been a salesman's sample. *Authors' collection.*

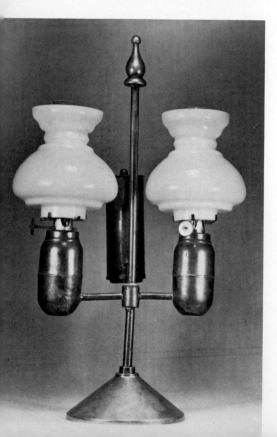

Fig. 84. Brass student lamp; on base "Pat. Oct. 28 79"; milk glass shade; Nutmeg burner; 9½ inches to top of rod. Rodney *collection.*

Fig. 85. Brass student lamp with white Bristol shade; foreign burner; 8 inches to top of supporting rod. *Bankert collection.*

Fig. 86. Double student lamp in brass with white Bristol shades; foreign burners; 14¼ inches to top of supporting stand. *Bankert collection.*

66

Fig. 87. Brass log double student lamp; "Pat. Oct. 28—79"; milk glass shades with fired-on yellow paint; Nutmeg burners; 11¼ inches to top of center stand. *Luckenbill collection.*

Fig. 88. Brass double student lamp with font to the rear; milk glass shades with fired-on yellow paint; Nutmeg burner; 12 inches to top of center stand. *Luckenbill collection.*

Fig. 89. Brass double student lamp; pink painted milk glass shades; Nutmeg burners; 9 inches to top of center stand. *Wehle collection.*

67

Fig. 95. Brass lamp with brass shade; Acorn burner; 10½ inches high. The decoration on the brass shade is known as repoussé work and was very popular in the 1880s as an amateur art. It had a revival about 1907-1908 and it is possible that the lamp is of this later period. *Authors' collection*

Fig. 96. Peg lamp in brass candle-stick; clear glass font; brass shade with red cloth lining; Nutmeg burner; 13 inches high. *Schafer collection.*

Fig. 97. Brass lamp and shade with amber, green, and blue jewels; green beaded fringe on shade; for-eign burner; 8½ inches high. *Wehle collection.*

Fig. 98. Brass ribbed panels In lamp and shade; green, blue, and red jewels in shade; clear bead fringe around shade; foreign burner; 12¾ inches high. *Authors' collection.*

Fig. 99. Candle-holder lamp with brass base and red beaded shade; Acorn burner; 10½ inches high; made about 1905. *Authors' collection.*

Fig. 100. Brass base heavily embossed with barnyard scene, trees, chickens, goats, and a house; green cased glass shade; Nutmeg burner; 10 inches high. *Wehle collection.*

71

Fig. 101. Brass lamp with a green milk glass shade topped with a wide brass band; foreign burner; 7 inches high. *Authors' collection.*

Fig. 102. Brass pedestal base, green milk glass shade; foreign burner; 8¼ inches high. *Luckenbill collection.*

Fig. 103. Clear glass stem lamp with square base; Acorn burner; 4 inches high. In Butler Brothers' catalog "Our Drummer" for Apr. 1912 it is pictured and priced at 96¢ per dozen. *Authors' collection.*

Fig. 104. Clear glass stem lamp; Acorn burner; 5½ inches high. *Authors' collection.*

Fig. 105. Clear glass stem lamp; Nutmeg burner; 5 inches high. *Plasterer collection.*

Fig. 106. Clear glass embossed block stem lamp; Nutmeg burner; 5¼ inches high. *Plasterer collection.*

73

Fig. 107. Clear glass with paneled font and pedestal base; Nutmeg burner; 5½ inches high. *Authors' collection.*

Fig. 108. Clear glass with embossed "hemstitched" heart-shaped alternate panels frosted and decorated with painted flowers; paint badly worn; Acorn burner; 5½ inches high. In Butler Brothers' catalog "Our Drummer" for Feb. 1900 it is listed as "Heart Pattern" and priced at $1.30 per dozen. *Authors' collection.*

Fig. 109. Green glass in embossed Beaded Heart pattern; Acorn burner; 5½ inches high. Found also in clear glass and in clear glass with frosted hearts. *Authors' collection.*

74

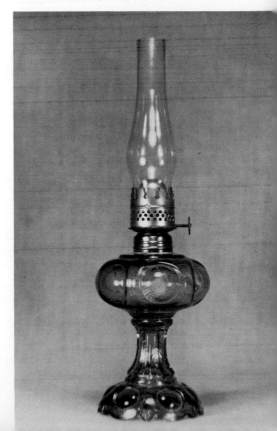

Fig. 110. Clear glass stem lamp; this pattern often called Bull's-eye; molded in glass around collar "Patented Sept. 19 & Nov. 14, 1911," which apparently refers to the collar; Acorn burner; 5¾ inches high. Also found with red bull's-eyes and completely gilded. *Plasterer collection.*

Fig. 111. Blue glass with embossed pattern similar to the Bull's-eye; Nutmeg burner; 5 inches high. *Authors' collection.*

Fig. 112. Embossed amber glass lamp; Nutmeg burner; 5 inches high. Found also in blue and in clear glass. In Butler Brothers' catalog "Our Drummer" for Apr. 1912 it is listed as "Daisy" with "large bull's-eye foot and shoulder, colonial stem" and was priced at 95¢ per dozen. *Authors' collection.*

75

Fig. 113. **Clear glass stem lamp with embossed medallions; Acorn burner; 5½ inches high.** *Authors' collection.*

Fig. 114. **Green glass pedestal lamp with embossed flowers; Acorn burner; 5½ inches high.** Found also in blue, clear glass, and in clear glass with frosted font and flowers. *Authors' collection.*

Fig. 115. **Clear glass stem lamp with embossed design and frosted font; Acorn burner; 5½ inches high.** *Authors' collection.*

Fig. 116. Fish-scale pattern in blue glass; Nutmeg burner; 5 inches high. Found also in amber, green, vaseline, and clear glass. *Authors' collection.*

Fig. 117. Amber glass in Waffle pattern with brass pedestal base; Acorn burner; 4½ inches high. Found also in blue and in clear glass. *Authors' collection.*

Fig. 118. Vaseline stem lamp with embossed pattern on font; sometimes called Buckle pattern; Nutmeg burner; 5½ inches high. Found also in blue glass. *Authors' collection.*

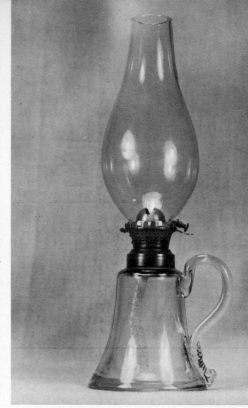

Fig. 119. Clear glass in a swirl pattern with molded threads for the screw-on collar; Acorn burner; 8¼ inches to top of swirl chimney. This lamp filled with perfumed oil was sold in the 1920s and 1930s, if not later. *Authors' collection.*

Fig. 120. Clear glass with applied handle; on burner "Holmes, Booth & Haydens. Patent Jan. 24, 1860"; 11 inches high. *Authors' collection.*

Fig. 121. Crystal "Acorn" lamp; clear paneled glass with embossed acorn cup; Acorn burner; 4 inches high. Found also in milk and in crystal striped glass and in mercury glass in both gold and silver. *Authors' collection.*

Fig. 122. Milk glass, almost opalescent, with embossed grapes and leaves; Acorn burner; 3¼ inches high. Pictured in "Our Drummer" of Butler Brothers, New York, for Apr. 1912, at 92¢ per dozen. They are also seen in pairs as salt and pepper shakers. Peterson calls it Four-sided Grape pattern. *Clark collection.*

Fig. 123. Milk glass lamp with embossed grapes and leaves; on either side, salt and pepper shakers in the same pattern but painted reddish and gold in the "Goofus" manner; this paint is not fired and is readily removed; the lamp may have been painted at one time; Acorn burner; 3¼ inches high. *Authors' collection.*

79

Fig. 124. Pair of milk glass lamps, one with orange ground, the other with green, both with colorful flowers and matching shades; on either side are salt and pepper shakers in matching colors; Acorn burner; 6¾ inches high. *Plasterer collection.*

Fig. 125. *Left:* Milk glass in embossed pattern with painted gold ribs. *Right:* Clear glass in same pattern. *Center:* Same base as a salt shaker. Acorn burner lamps; 6¾ inches high. Miniature lamp collectors call this the Christmas Tree pattern but Peterson in his salt shaker book calls it Shag. In Butler Brothers' catalog "Our Drummer" for Apr. 1912 it is pictured and priced at 93¢ per dozen. *Authors' collection.*

Fig. 126. Left: Milk glass in ribbed and paneled pattern and badly worn purple flowers. *Right:* Clear glass in same pattern. *Center:* Same base as a salt shaker. Acorn burner; lamps 6¾ inches high. This base was threaded about the top and served a double purpose. Equipped with a matching chimney-shade and a burner, it was a lamp; supplied with perforated tops, a pair of them served as salt and pepper shakers. *Authors' collection.*

Fig. 127. Pewter pedestal base; clear class embossed ribbed panel font and shade; Acorn burner; 8½ inches high. *Authors' collection.*

Fig. 128. Pewter pedestal base; font and shade in milk glass with ribs; Acorn burner; 7¾ inches high. Found also painted in various patterns, but since the paint is not fired on, it is usually badly worn. *Authors' collection.*

Fig. 129. Milk glass, ribbed panels; nasturtium flowers and leaves in yellow, orange, and green; ribs and top and bottom of shade and base gilted; P. & A. Victor burner; 10 inches high. *Rodney collection.*

Fig. 130. Milk glass, ribbed panels, trimmed in gold; floral decorations in blue and pink; paint not fired on; Nutmeg burner; 7¼ inches high. Also found without decoration or gold trimming. *Wehle collection.*

82

Fig. 131. Clear glass with embossed beaded swirl with flowers and leaves in panels; Hornet burner; 8½ inches high. *Authors' collection.*

Fig. 132. Clear glass with embossed flowers, leaves, and scrolls; Hornet burner; 8 inches high. *Authors' collection.*

Fig. 133. Clear glass in Diamond pattern with embossed flowers; Acorn burner; 6¾ inches high. *Authors' collection.*

Fig. 134. Clear glass with embossed flowers and other decoration; painted all over red, but paint badly worn; Acorn burner; 6¾ inches high. *Authors' collection.*

Fig. 135. Clear glass with embossed flowers and leaves; painted red all over, resembling red satin glass; Acorn burner; 7¼ inches high. *Authors' collection.*

Fig. 136. Clear glass with embossed panels in Diamond pattern; Acorn burner; 7 inches high. *Bartol collection.*

84

Fig. 137. Pewter pedestal base; ribbed panel clear glass font and shade with embossed flowers and leaves painted gold; Acorn burner; 7¾ inches high. *Authors' collection.*

Fig. 138. Clear glass with embossed bands painted red; paint not fired on; Hornet burner; 8 inches high. Found also in green glass with gilt bands. *Authors' collection.*

Fig. 139. Clear glass embossed with lilies; ground painted green, flowers red and gold (probably repainted); Hornet burner; 9 inches high. *Authors' collection.*

85

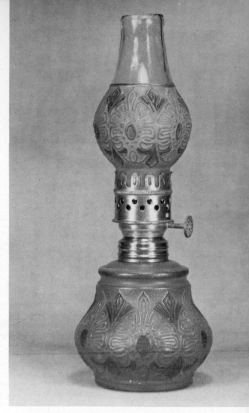

Fig. 140. Clear glass with embossed beaded swirl and flowers; painted light green with red flowers and green leaves (possibly repainted); Hornet burner; 8½ inches high. *Authors' collection.*

Fig. 141. Clear embossed glass painted in reddish trimmed in green; Nutmeg burner; 7½ inches high. Found also painted in greenish blue, pale blue trimmed in gold, and in pale pink. *Authors' collection.*

Fig. 142. Clear glass in Hobnail pattern, painted light pink; paint not fired on; screw-on collar; Nutmeg burner; 8¼ inches high. *Myers collection.*

Fig. 143. "Lincoln Drape" lamp; clear glass textured and embossed; Acorn burner; 5¾ inches high. Purchased about 1938 at McCrory's for $1.00. *Authors' collection.*

Fig. 144. Westmoreland pattern; clear pressed glass made by Gillinder and Sons at Greensburg, Pa., about 1889. (It was named for Westmoreland County, Pa., in which the company's pressed glass department was located; it was also called No. 420). Acorn burner; 7½ inches high. *Authors' collection.*

Fig. 145. Clear pressed glass in Westmoreland pattern (see Fig. 144); Nutmeg burner; 8½ inches high. *Authors' collection.*

Fig. 146. Clear pressed glass, West-moreland pattern (see Fig. 144), encased in silver filigree; Nutmeg burner; 10 inches high. *Authors' collection.*

Fig. 147. Clear pressed glass; font resembles pears, saucer of base matches shade; Hornet burner; 9¼ inches high. *Authors' collection.*

Fig. 148. Pressed clear glass base and shade, partly frosted; Nutmeg burner; 6¾ inches high. See also Fig. 151. *Authors' collection.*

Fig. 149. Same lamp as shown in Fig. 150, unassembled.

Fig. 150. Bull's-eye pattern (variation) in clear glass; Nutmeg burner; 7¾ inches high. Made by United States Glass Co., Pittsburgh, Pa., as their pattern No. 151. See also Fig. 149. *Authors' collection.*

Fig. 151. Pressed clear glass base and shade; partly frosted; Nutmeg burner; 6¼ inches high. See also Fig. 148. *Ritter collection.*

Fig. 152. Clear glass with pressed rose design painted in rose and gold; Hornet burner; 12¼ inches high. This type of glass is usually painted but since the paint was not fired on, it is often partly or entirely missing. This glass is usually called "Goofus glass" today. *Authors' collection.*

Fig. 153. Milk glass with green painted ground; embossed flowers and designs trimmed in gilt; Acorn burner; 9½ inches high. Found also in unpainted clear glass. *Rodney collection.*

Fig. 154. Clear glass, embossed flowers and scrolls; the square base is painted gold; Acorn burner; 9 inches high. *Reinert collection.*

90

Fig. 155. Clear glass with embossed flowers and scrolls; Acorn burner; 8¼ inches high. *Authors' collection.*

Fig. 156. Milk glass embossed with flowers and scrolls; pink, brown, and gold paint not fired on and badly worn; Acorn burner; 8 inches high. Found also with blue and gold paint. Called "Jupiter" and pictured in Butler Brothers' catalog "Our Drummer" for Apr. 1912 at 89¢ per dozen. These bases are also found in pairs with perforated tops as salt and pepper shakers. *Authors' collection.*

Fig. 157. Milk glass painted blue, embossed scrolling and flowers gilted in gold, paint badly worn; Hornet burner; 8¾ inches high. *Funderwhite collection.*

Fig. 158. Milk glass with embossed flowers and designs; pink shading around top of shade and bottom of base; painted floral decorations in blue, yellow, and green; Hornet burner; 7½ inches high. *Bartol collection.*

Fig. 159. Milk glass with embossed scrolls; painted flowers in red and green are badly worn; Hornet burner; 7½ inches high. *Authors' collection.*

Fig. 160. Milk glass; embossed scrolling painted in red, brown, and gold; Hornet burner; 7½ inches high. *Authors' collection.*

Fig. 161. Milk glass with embossed design and flowers; ground color brown, flowers pink, and trim gold; Hornet burner; 8½ inches high. Also found with ground painted green. *Clark collection.*

Fig. 162. Milk glass; embossed flowers and leaves gilted in gold; Hornet burner; 8¼ inches high. *Lindemuth collection.*

Fig. 163. Mug lamp in Gothic Arch pattern; embossed milk glass with removable font; matching milk glass chimney; Acorn burner; 7¾ inches high. See also Fig. 164. *Authors' collection.*

Fig. 164. Tumbler lamp in Gothic Arch pattern; embossed clear glass trimmed in gilt; removable font may be lifted out; Acorn burner; 7 inches high. The shade is identical to that in Fig. 165. *Authors' collection.*

Fig. 165. Gothic Arch pattern, embossed clear glass decorated in gold; Acorn burner; 6¾ inches high. We have seen this lamp several times and apparently the base and shade match. See Fig. 164. *Authors' collection.*

Fig. 166. Grecian Key lamp; embossed clear glass; Acorn burner; 8½ inches high. Found also painted an all-over red, but paint not fired on and partly missing. This lamp derives its name from the band of Greek fret embossed on shade and font. The lamps shown in Figs. 167, 168, and 169 have the same pattern. *Authors' collection.*

94

Fig. 167. Grecian Key lamp; embossed clear glass; Acorn burner; 7¾ inches high. Date in glass around collar "Patented Sept. 19 & Nov. 14, 1911." Found also in green glass. *Authors' collection.*

Fig. 168. Grecian Key lamp; embossed clear glass; Acorn burner; 6¾ inches high. *Authors' collection.*

Fig. 169. Grecian Key lamp; embossed milk glass with painted orchid flowers; paint partly worn off; Acorn burner; 6 inches high. *Authors' collection.*

Fig. 170. Rose-like pattern; milk glass saucer base with matching clear glass chimney-shade; traces of gilt remain; Acorn burner; 6¾ inches high. *Authors' collection.*

Fig. 171. Clear glass with embossed pond lilies painted in red and gold; Acorn burner; 6 inches high. *Authors' collection.*

Fig. 172. Milk glass with embossed flowers and other designs; painted in reddish brown with flowers in red and gold; paint not fired on; Acorn burner; 6 inches high. Pictured in Butler Brothers' catalog "Our Drummer" for Apr. 30, 1912; came in assorted colors at 96¢ per dozen. *Authors' collection.*

96

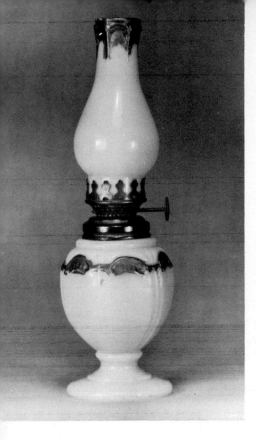

Fig. 173. Milk glass with embossed design on both lamp and chimney; gold gilt badly worn; Acorn burner; 7¾ inches high. *Authors' collection.*

Fig. 174. Milk glass in a swirl pattern with gold gilt decoration; Nutmeg burner; 9¾ inches high to top of chimney. *Authors' collection.*

Fig. 175. Paneled milk glass painted blue; flowers red with green leaves; Acorn burner; 7 inches high. *Authors' collection.*

97

Fig. 176. Milk glass with embossed ribs; Acorn burner; 6½ inches high. *Bartol collection.*

Fig. 177. Custard glass with embossed design; Acorn burner; 6 inches high. Found also in blue, white, and deep pink milk glass. Called "Leon's Ribbed" in Warman's *Antiques,* 6th ed. In C. M. Linnington's catalog "Silent Salesman" for Jan. 1894 it is pictured and listed as "Quarter-Dollar Leader Lamp." They sold for $1.00 per dozen and came in ivory, white, and blue. The catalog adds: "The dealer that can't sell this for a quarter each would be unable to give goods away." See also Fig. 178. *Authors' collection.*

Fig. 178. Blue milk glass with embossed design and covered with silver filigree; Acorn burner; 6 inches high. See also Fig. 177. *Schafer collection.*

Fig. 179. Blue milk glass; embossed beaded panels; Acorn burner; 7 Inches high. Also found in clear blue, amber, and green. *Ritter collection.*

Fig. 180. Milk glass with embossed beaded panels; Nutmeg burner; 8 inches high. *Sullivan collection.*

Fig. 181. Blue milk glass; applied handle; foreign burner; 5¼ inches high. Also found in pink opalescent glass. *Schafer collection.*

99

Fig. 182. White Bristol glass with embossed ribbing at top of base and top of shade; Hornet burner; 7¼ inches high. *Authors' collection.*

Fig. 183. Milk glass; embossed beading in gold, flowers pink and green, orange trim at top of shade and base; paint poorly fired on; Hornet burner; 10 inches high. *Reinert collection.*

Fig. 184. Milk glass with embossed plain and beaded panels and design; Hornet burner; 8½ inches high. Also found with various painted designs. *Authors' collection.*

Fig. 185. Embossed milk glass with yellow and pink fired-on flowers; Hornet burner; 9 inches high. Luckenbill collection.

Fig. 186. Milk glass painted with a satin egg-shell finish; enameled flowers in red, white, and brown; Acorn burner; 7½ inches high. Authors' collection.

Fig. 187. Milk glass; paneled base and egg-shaped shade; embossed scrolling painted green; paint not fired on; Acorn burner; 6½ inches high. Also found with scrolling in yellow. Bates collection.

Fig. 188. Milk glass with embossed ribbed panels; pink around top of shade and base; Nutmeg burner; 7 inches high. See Fig. 189. *Bartol collection.*

Fig. 189. Milk glass with wide embossed ribs; painted blue shading to white; Nutmeg burner; 7 inches high. Found also in yellow shading to white and in pink shading to white. See Fig. 188. *Authors' collection.*

Fig. 190. Milk glass with embossed Block and Dot pattern; Acorn burner; 7½ inches high. Found also with painted outlines and in clear glass. Found also with an umbrella shade. See Fig. 191. *Authors' collection.*

Fig. 191. Milk glass with embossed Block and Dot pattern outlined in mahogany; Acorn burner; 7 inches high. Found also in clear glass stained a light green with gold outlines. Found also with ball shade. See Fig. 190. *Authors' collection.*

Fig. 192. Milk glass with embossed design; decorated with gilt and flowers in blue and green, partly worn off; Acorn burner; 6½ inches high. Pictured as "Mission" design in Butler Brothers' catalog "Our Drummer" of Apr. 30, 1912, and priced at 95¢ per dozen. *Authors' collection.*

Fig. 193. Milk glass with embossed pattern and flowers; pale pink around top of base and shade; flowers in pink, orchid, and green; Acorn burner; 7 inches high. Sometimes called "Apple Blossom." See Fig. 194. *Authors' collection.*

Fig. 194. Milk glass with embossed flowers and beading; light green band around top of base and shade and pink and green flower decorations; Nutmeg burner; 7¼ inches high. Sometimes called "Apple Blossom." See Fig. 193. *Authors' collection.*

Fig. 195. Milk glass with embossed net swirl and flowers; flowers pink with green leaves, paint fired on; Nutmeg burner; 6¼ inches high. This pattern is sometimes called "Apple Blossom." *Plasterer collection.*

Fig. 196. Milk glass with embossed rims around top of base and top and bottom of shade which are painted green; painted flowers are red, pink, and green; Nutmeg burner; 6½ inches high. Found also with pink trim and in green milk glass. *Authors' collection.*

Fig. 197. Milk glass, leaf embossed base and ribbed shade painted in blue, green, and gold, which is worn; Acorn burner; 5¾ inches high. This is the "Kenova Night Lamp," made by the Fostoria Glass Co., Mountsville, W. Va., about 1890. *Authors' collection.*

Fig. 198. Paneled milk glass with embossed flowers; sprayed with shades of brown and green paint, not fired on; Hornet burner; 7½ inches high. *Authors' collection.*

Fig. 199. Milk glass with embossed designs; geometric designs covered with gold dust; flowers and other designs in red, green, and black, paint badly worn; Hornet burner; 8¾ inches high. *Authors' collection.*

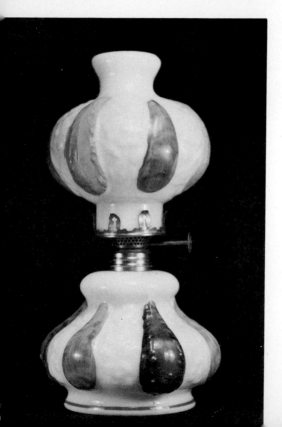

Fig. 200. Milk glass with embossed scrolling painted in red, brown, and gold; Hornet burner; 8½ inches high. *Authors' collection.*

Fig. 201. Milk glass in a swirl pattern with embossed roses and scrolls; fired-on orange decoration; Hornet burner; 10½ inches high. Found also with decorations in other colors. *Authors' collection.*

Fig. 202. Milk glass with embossed panels, panels painted alternately blue and orange-red; Hornet burner; 8½ inches high. Sometimes called "Centennial Lamp." *Authors' collection.*

Fig. 203. Milk glass in Plume pattern with gilt decorations; Nutmeg burner; 7½ inches high. Now reproduced in several colors. *Authors' collection.*

Fig. 204. Clear glass with embossed Iris pattern; flowers and leaves painted gold, somewhat worn; Hornet burner; 9 inches high. See Fig. 205. *Authors' collection.*

Fig. 205. Milk glass with embossed Iris pattern; flowers and leaves decorated with gold gilt; Acorn burner; 7¼ inches high. Found also in clear glass decorated in gold and in milk glass painted greenish. See Fig. 204. *Authors' collection.*

107

Fig. 206. Milk glass, embossed, multi-colored decorations; Nutmeg burner; 8 inches high. Usually called ''Sunflower.'' *Authors' collection.*

Fig. 207. Milk glass with embossed design and flowers; flowers yellow with green leaves; Nutmeg burner; 8 inches high. *Zies collection.*

Fig. 208. Milk glass with embossed design and flowers; only traces of green, yellow, and gold paint remain; Nutmeg burner; 7¼ inches high. See Fig. 209. *Authors' collection.*

Fig. 209. Milk glass with embossed design and flowers; pansies are orange, pink, and yellow with green leaves, all badly worn; Nutmeg burner; 9¼ inches high. See Fig. 208. *Authors' collection.*

Fig. 210. Milk glass; embossed design gilted; painted birds and flowers on one side, house and bridge on the other; paint poorly fired on; Hornet burner; 9 inches high. *Plasterer collection.*

Fig. 211. Milk glass with embossed medallion and design; decorated with gilt now badly worn; Hornet burner; 9½ inches high. *Authors' collection.*

109

Fig. 212. Deep pink milk glass embossed with shells; Hornet burner; 9¾ inches high. Found also in blue milk glass. Called "Our 'Little Beauty' Night Lamp" in C. M. Linnington's catalog "Silent Salesman" for Jan. 1894. *Authors' collection.*

Fig. 213. Milk glass with embossed swirl and flowers; upper part of base and shade painted pink, flowers are yellow; Hornet burner; 9 inches high. Found also with green trim and pink flowers and in red satin glass. Often called "Chrysanthemum" pattern. *Authors' collection.*

Fig. 214. Milk glass with embossed Maltese Cross and other patterns; remains of gilt decoration still present; Hornet burner; 9½ inches high. Found also in milk glass painted all-over yellow; paint not fired on. Made by Eagle Glass & Mfg. Co., Wellsburg, W. Va., about 1894. *Authors' collection.*

110

Fig. 215. Custard glass with embossed beaded panels and boats, windmill, and lighthouse; Hornet burner; 7¾ inches high. Found also in pink, white, and blue milk glass. *Authors' collection.*

Fig. 216. Custard glass, swirl ribbing around base and shade; Hornet burner; 8 inches high. Found also in milk glass in white, yellow, and pink. *Bates collection.*

Fig. 217. Brady's Night Lamp; green milk glass with embossed design; Nutmeg burner; 7¾ inches high. Found also in a satin finish and in pink, blue, and white milk glass. Made by Consolidated Lamp and Glass Co., Pittsburgh, Pa., and shown in their catalog for 1894. *Authors' collection.*

Fig. 218. Milk glass with fired-on paint to resemble satin glass in white with pink shadings; vines in brown and pink; instead of a metal tripod, there is a round clear glass shade-holder which fits into the burner and holds the umbrella-type shade; Hornet burner; 9¼ inches high. *Authors' collection.*

Fig. 219. Milk glass base and clear shade; upper part of shade is painted white to resemble frosting; upper part of both base and shade have orange ground; floral sprays in white, yellow, and green; Hornet burner; 9 inches high. Found also with decorations in other colors and in blue glass. Usually called the "Nellie Bly" lamp. *Authors' collection.*

Fig. 220. Milk glass in raised panel design; fired-on paint pink shading to white with violets in purple and

112

green; Hornet burner; 8 inches high. Found also in orange satin glass. *Authors' collection.*

Fig. 221. Blue milk glass with embossed design which is trimmed with gilt; Hornet burner; 9¾ inches high. *Authors' collection.*

Fig. 222. Milk glass in embossed design and beaded corners; all-over yellow fired-on paint; Hornet burner; 9¾ inches high. *Plasterer collection.*

Fig. 223. Milk glass; gilded embossed designs, gilt partly worn off; Acorn burner; 6¾ inches high. Made by Eagle Glass and Mfg. Co., Wellsburg, W. Va. *Plasterer collection.*

113

Fig. 224. Milk glass with embossed wreaths; design and flowers in pink, green, and gold paint, poorly fired on; Nutmeg burner; 7¾ inches high. *Agnew collection.*

Fig. 225. Milk glass; embossed decorations and flowers painted in yellow, brown, and gold; Nutmeg burner; 8½ inches high. *Lindemuth collection.*

Fig. 226. Milk glass with embossed scrolling in gilt; flowers in red, yellow, brown, and green paint are badly worn; Acorn burner; 7¾ inches high. *Authors' collection.*

114

Fig. 227. Milk glass with embossed designs painted green; P. & A. Victor burner; 10 inches high. *Rodney collection.*

Fig. 228. Milk glass with embossed fleur-de-lis and other decorations painted in burgundy and gold; paint badly worn; Acorn burner; 7 inches high. Found also in clear glass. *Authors' collection.*

Fig. 229. Milk glass with embossed design and flowers; fired-on paint is pink, blue, and green; Nutmeg burner; 7½ inches high. Found also in both blue and green milk glass. *Authors' collection.*

115

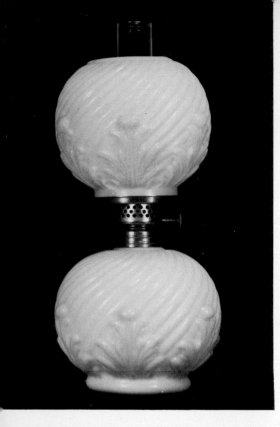

Fig. 230. Acanthus Lamp. Milk glass in a ribbed swirl with embossed acanthus leaf decorations in pink; Nutmeg burner; 8¼ inches high. Found also with decorations in yellow and in green. *Authors' collection.*

Fig. 231. Milk glass with shadings of fired-on blue paint; Nutmeg burner; 8½ inches high. Found also in milk glass with purple shadings and in satin glass in red, light green, light blue, and in light and dark pink. Often called "Drape" pattern. *Authors' collection.*

Fig. 232. Milk glass with embossed design, blue trimmed with pink and green flowers; Nutmeg burner; 8¼ inches high. *Luckenbill collection.*

116

Fig. 233. Blue milk glass with embossed design; probably a foreign lamp with Nutmeg burner; 8 inches high. *Wehle collection.*

Fig. 234. Blue milk glass with embossed design; Nutmeg burner; 8½ inches high. Found also in white and green milk glass. *Authors' collection.*

Fig. 235. Blue milk glass with embossed design; foreign burner; 7¼ inches high. *Wehle collection.*

117

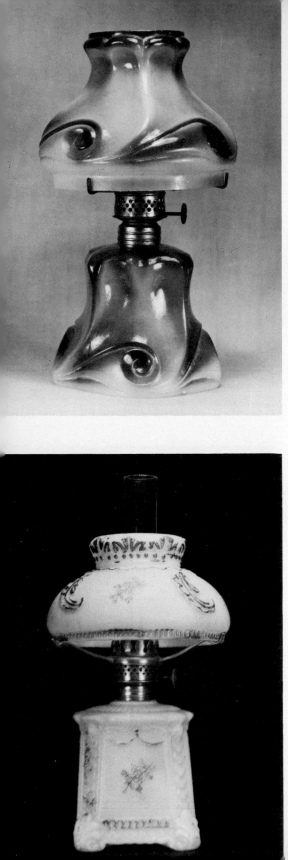

Fig. 242. Milk glass with embossed swirl design; painted ground greenish mustard ornamented in reddish purple; this was said to be the "Snail" pattern; Nutmeg burner; 8 inches high. *Zies collection.*

Fig. 243. Milk glass with embossed design with traces of gilt remaining; Nutmeg burner; 7½ inches high. *Authors' collection.*

Fig. 244. Milk glass with embossed design; gold painted flowers and decorations somewhat worn off; Nutmeg burner; 8 inches high. Called "Nara" night lamp and pictured in the Dodd, Werner, & Co. catalog for 1896-97 and listed at $8.00 per dozen or 80¢ each. *Authors' collection.*

120

Fig. 245. Milk glass with embossed design; gold painted flowers and decorations somewhat worn off; Nutmeg burner; 7¾ inches high. Found also in bluish white almost opalescent glass. Called "Elsie" night lamp and pictured in Dodd, Werner, & Co. catalog for 1896-97 at $8.00 per dozen or 80¢ each. *Authors' collection.*

Fig. 246. Milk glass with embossed shell and other ornaments; yellow ground with gold, pink, and blue decorations; nickel holder; Nutmeg burner; 7½ inches high. In Dodd, Werner, & Co. (Cincinnati, Ohio) catalog of 1896-97 it is called "Erminie" night lamp and priced at $10.00 per dozen or 90¢ each. *Wehle collection.*

Fig. 247. Milk glass with embossed design; flowers in blue and pink but paint not fired on; Nutmeg burner; 7½ inches high. *Authors' collection.*

Fig. 248. Hanging lamp; brass hanger holds embossed font and shade painted in delicate blue, yellow, pink, and gold; paint not fired on well; clear glass prisms; Acorn burner; 11½ inches to top of hanger. Found also in various colors, without prisms, and with a brass font. Called "Victoria" night lamp and pictured in Butler Brothers' catalog "Our Drummer" for Feb. 1900, priced at $1.00 each. See also Fig. 249. *Authors' collection.*

Fig. 249. Hanging lamp; shade is milk glass with embossed shells in delicate pink and blue trimmed in gold; font and chain are brass; foreign burner; 11¾ inches to top of chain. See also Fig. 248. *Clark collection.*

Fig. 250. Milk glass with embossed design; painted in delicate blue, pink, and gold somewhat worn off;

122

We hope that you enjoy this book… and that it will occupy a proud place in your library. We would like to keep you informed about other publications from Schiffer. Simply fill in and mail this postage-free card today.

TITLE OF BOOK: _____

☐ hardcover
☐ paperback

☐ Bought at: _____
☐ Received as gift

COMMENTS: _____

☐ *Please add my name to your mailing list to receive information about books on:*

1. ☐ Porcelain
2. ☐ Photography
3. ☐ Gardening
4. ☐ Metal
5. ☐ Self help
6. ☐ Dolls

7. ☐ Architecture
8. ☐ Nature
9. ☐ Cooking
10. ☐ Decoys
11. ☐ Glass
12. ☐ Antique furniture

☐ *Please send me a FREE copy of the latest catalog of Schiffer Books.*

Name _____
Address _____
City _____ State _____ Zip _____

SCHIFFER BOOKS ARE CURRENTLY AVAILABLE FROM YOUR BOOKSE

Printed in U.S.A.

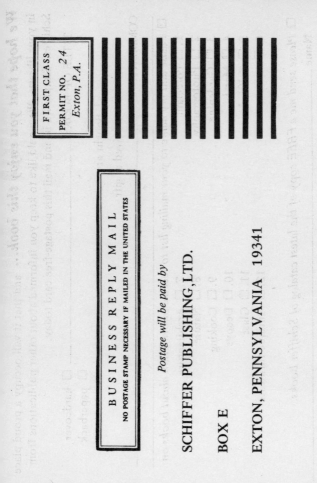

Nutmeg burner; 7¾ inches high. Called "Diana" in Dodd, Werner, & Co. catalog for 1896-97 at $8.00 per dozen or 80¢ each. *Authors' collection.*

Fig. 251. Hanging lamp in white metal washed in brass; white Bristol shade; foreign burner; 6½ inches to top of chain. *Luckenbill collection.*

Fig. 252. Brass hanging lamp; ribbed pink cased glass shade; cut crystal prisms; Nutmeg burner; 22½ inches to top of chain. *Authors' collection.*

Fig. 253. Hanging lamp; pressed brass bracket holds embossed milk glass lamp painted in delicate blues, yellow, and gold; brass reflector; Acorn burner; 2¾ inches high. *Authors' collection.*

123

Fig. 254. Clear glass with ground painted in bronze; embossed grapes and leaves gilted in gold; paint not fired and somewhat worn; Acorn burner; 7¼ inches high. Found also painted green with gold grapes and leaves. *Authors' collection.*

Fig. 255. Milk glass with embossed pattern; gold gilt partly missing; Nutmeg burner; 8 inches high. Found also in blue milk glass and in greenish vaseline glass. This base also found with a matching globe shade. See Fig. 257. *Authors' collection.*

Fig. 256. Pewter pedestal base; milk glass with embossed grapes and leaves; gilted in gold which is badly worn off; Acorn burner; 8¼ inches high. Found also painted in pink with gold decorations. *Authors' collection.*

Fig. 257. Light custard glass with embossed pattern; gold gilt partly missing; Hornet burner; 9 inches high. Found also in blue, green, and blue opalescent glass painted in various ways. Paint is not fired on and is usually worn. This base also found with a matching umbrella shade. See Fig. 255. *Authors' collection.*

Fig. 258. Amethyst glass, embossed design; Hornet burner; 9¾ inches high. *Lindemuth collection.*

Fig. 259. Pewter pedestal base; frosted clear glass; embossed grapes and leaves painted orange and gold in fired-on paint; Acorn burner; 8½ inches high. *Plasterer collection.*

125

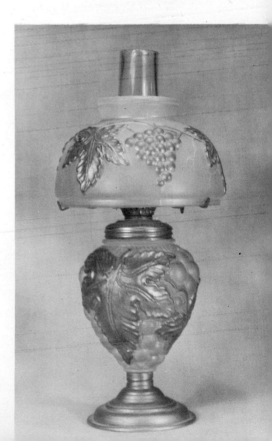

Fig. 260. Cobalt blue glass with embossed design; gilt decorations badly worn; Hornet burner; 8¾ inches high. *Authors' collection.*

Fig. 261. Blue glass, embossed design gilted in gold, not fired on and badly worn off; Hornet burner; 9½ inches high. *Plasterer collection.*

Fig. 262. Custard glass in paneled and embossed design, trimmed in dark brown and gold; paint badly worn; Hornet burner; 9 inches high. Found also in crystal, blue, and amethyst glass trimmed in various colors of paint. *Authors' collection.*

Fig. 263. Embossed blue milk glass; Hornet burner; 8½ inches high. *Luckenbill collection.*

Fig. 264. Milk glass with fine, cloth-like texture and embossed ribs; top of shade and top and bottom of base light blue, flowers red, and leaves green; Nutmeg burner; 8¼ inches high. *Myers collection.*

Fig. 265. Milk glass with embossed pattern; painted green shading to light green in fired-on paint; Nutmeg burner; 8¼ inches high. Found also with painted floral decorations. *Authors' collection.*

Fig. 266. Milk glass with embossed design; painted blue around top of base and shade, pansies in yellow, red, and orchid with green leaves; Nutmeg burner; 9½ inches high. Found also trimmed in orange with blue bellflowers. *Authors' collection.*

Fig. 267. Embossed milk glass; dots, ribs, and bands with painted blue decoration, green vine with pink buds; in blue, green, and pink; foreign burner; 7½ inches high. *Bartol collection.*

Fig. 268. Milk glass with embossed ornamentation; yellow trim at top of shade and at bottom of base, also purple and green floral sprays; embossed lions' heads are gilted; Nutmeg burner; 8½ inches high. *Authors' collection.*

Fig. 269. Milk glass with embossed feather-like pattern and saucer base; Acorn burner; 7¾ inches high. *Authors collection.*

Fig. 270. Milk glass with an embossed design; fired-on painted blue forget-me-nots with green leaves; on shade "Compliments of Jack Hart"; Acorn burner; 7¼ inches high. Jack Hart was a clothing-store owner in Washington, Pa., many years ago and apparently these lamps were given to customers. *Authors' collection.*

Fig. 271. Milk glass with embossed design; painted with green shadings and leaves; Nutmeg burner; 8 inches high. Found also with orange flowers and green leaves. *Authors' collection.*

Fig. 272. Milk glass embossed with an orange-skin texture and a design; fired-on paint in brown; Nutmeg burner; 8½ inches high. Found also painted in blue and in red. *Authors' collection.*

Fig. 273. Milk glass with embossed design with fired-on paint in pink and green; Nutmeg burner; 8¾ inches high. Also found painted in yellow and pink and in red satin glass. *Authors' collection.*

Fig. 274. Milk glass with embossed design; fired-on green paint; Nutmeg burner; 7¾ inches high. Found also with reddish paint. *Authors' collection.*

Fig. 275. *(on facing page)* Eagle lamp; milk glass with embossed decorations; yellow and blue painted ground with eagles and other decorations in gilt; Nutmeg burner; 7½

inches high. Found also with ground painted in orange and brick red and in green and white, both with gilt decorations. We saw one in un-painted milk glass but suspect that the paint had been removed since it is always poorly fired on. In Butler Brothers' catalog "Our Drummer" for Feb. 1900 this lamp is priced at $2.25 per dozen. *Authors' collection.*

Fig. 276. Milk glass with fired-on brown paint; Nutmeg burner; 7¼ inches high. Found also in green milk glass and in clear green glass decorated with gilt. Often called "Pineapple in a Basket" pattern. *Authors' collection.*

Fig. 277. Basket Weave lamp; milk glass with embossed basket weave trimmed in gold gilt; Acorn burner; 6½ inches high. Found also painted green and gold. *Authors' collection.*

Fig. 278. Basket lamp; milk glass with embossed basket of flowers; basket and ribbon painted brown, flowers in assorted colors; paint not fired on and badly worn; Acorn burner, 7½ inches high. Found also in clear glass painted white and pink with basket and flowers in different colors. *Authors' collection.*

Fig. 279. Yellow cased glass with embossed design; Nutmeg burner; 7½ inches high. Made by Consolidated Lamp and Glass Co., Pittsburgh, Pa., and called "Basket Lamp" in their 1894 catalog. Found also in pink cased glass and in yellow and blue satin glass. *Authors' collection.*

Fig. 280. Milk glass in a draped pattern with a very rough finish; pink mottled with white in fired-on paint; Nutmeg burner; 9 inches high. *Authors' collection.*

Fig. 281. Shell pattern in milk glass; rough finish; brown and gold paint not fired on and partly worn off; Hornet burner; 9 inches high. Also found painted silver and gold and in smooth finish. *Bartol collection.*

Fig. 282. Blue milk glass with embossed flowers; Nutmeg burner; 7¼ inches high. Found also in both light and dark pink and in white milk glass. *Authors' collection.*

Fig. 283. Milk glass with embossed beads and scrolling; fired-on painted flowers in red and green and green beads; Nutmeg burner; 8¼ inches high. *Authors' collection.*

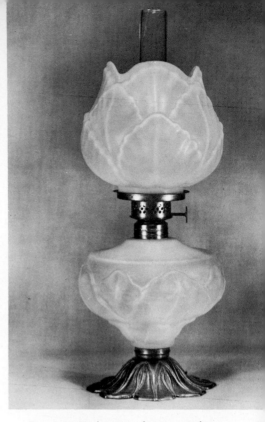

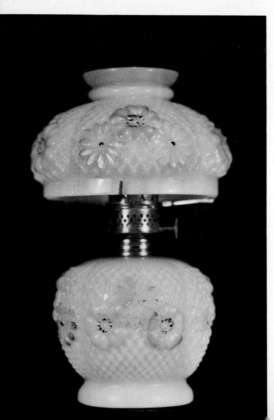

Fig. 284. Red satin glass; petal-type shade embossed and outlined with beading; base also has embossed deisgn; Nutmeg burner; 9 inches high. Found also in blue and in green satin glass. *Authors' collection.*

Fig. 285. Brass pedestal base; green opalescent glass with satin finish and embossed petal design; Nutmeg burner; 9½ inches high. Found also in both pink and red satin glass. *Authors' collection.*

Fig. 286. Milk glass with embossed design; fired-on paint is blue around top of base and shade, flowers are yellow, pink, and blue; Nutmeg burner; 7½ inches high. Also found with yellow or pink top and bottom. In cased glass it is found in yellow and pink. In clear glass it is found frosted or painted white to resemble milk glass, paint not fired on usually largely missing. There may have been unpainted ones also.

134

Westmoreland Specialty Co., Grapeville, Pa., called this pattern
"Daisy" in their 1890 catalog. It is
now commonly called "Cosmos."
Authors' collection.

Fig. 287. Tulip lamp; overshot glass
frosted inside, apricot shading to
clear; Nutmeg burner; 8½ inches
high. Found also in green shading
to clear and in pink shading to clear
in overshot; in green opalescent
shading to olive; in milk glass
painted green and pink; and in red
satin glass. *Authors' collection.*

Fig. 288. Red satin glass with embossed design; P. & A. Victor
burner; 11¾ inches high. Also
found in orange satin glass. *Schafer
collection.*

Fig. 289. Blue milk glass with embossed petal design; Hornet burner;
8½ inches high. Also found in
green and in pink milk glass. *Funderwhite collection.*

Fig. 290. Pink and white spatter glass in a swirl pattern with embossed fish net and flowers; Nutmeg burner; 6½ inches high. *Luckenbill collection.*

Fig. 291. Porcelain base in green, white, and gold with flowers in pink, blue, and brown; milk glass shade in matching colors, with scene; P. & A. Victor burner; 9¾ inches high. *Authors' collection.*

Fig. 292. Frosted clear glass with embossed scrolls, flowers, and a spider web barely visible; trimmed in gilt badly worn; Nutmeg burner; 8¼ inches high. Found also in red satin glass and in milk glass, the latter painted in various colors. The lamp is often called "Spider Web" pattern although the web usually does not show or is very indistinct. *Authors' collection.*

136

Fig. 293. Pink satin glass in a swirl pattern; enameled white daisies and green leaves; Nutmeg burner; 6½ inches high. Also found without flowers in blue satin glass, clear frosted glass, amber without satin finish, and orange iridescent glass. *Zies collection.*

Fig. 294. Spatter glass, honey color with off-white flecks in a swirl pattern; Nutmeg burner; 6¼ inches high. See Fig. 298. *Authors' collection.*

Fig. 295. Milk glass with embossed base; flowers painted in yellow and pink with green leaves; fired on; P. & A. Victor burner; 9¾ inches high. *Rodney collection.*

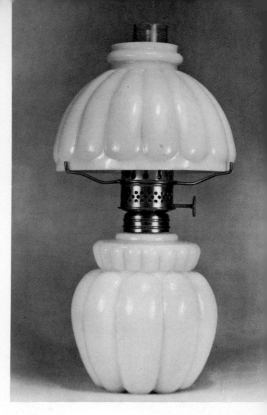

Fig. 296. Milk glass with pale pink fired-on paint around top of base and bottom of shade and blue flowers; melon ribbed; Nutmeg burner; 7¾ inches high. Found also with other decorations. In catalog of Westmoreland Specialty Co., Grapeville, Pa., about 1890, it was called ''Sylvan.'' See page 22. *Authors' collection.*

Fig. 297. Custard glass with embossed ribs; Nutmeg burner; 7¾ inches high. Found also in blue and in white milk glass. *Authors' collection.*

Fig. 298. Spatter glass, honey color with off-white flecks in a swirl pattern; completely covered with silver filigree; Nutmeg burner; 6¼ inches high. See Fig. 294. *Agnew collection.*

138

Fig. 299. Pea-green satin glass with embossed ribs; Nutmeg burner; 8½ inches high. Found also in blue and in white. See Figs. 300 and 301. *Authors' collection.*

Fig. 300. Light green satin glass with embossed ribs; fired-on flowers in purplish and yellow with green leaves; Nutmeg burner; 9 inches high. *Myers collection.*

Fig. 301. Milk glass, ribbed, covered with silver filigree; Nutmeg burner; 8¼ inches high. Also found in blue and light green satin glass without the filigree. *Plasterer collection.*

Fig. 302. Brass pedestal base; red satin glass in paneled pattern; Nutmeg burner; 9½ inches high. Found also in milk glass with painted decorations. See Fig. 303. *Authors' collection.*

Fig. 303. Brass pedestal base; milk glass in paneled pattern painted dark pink shading to white, flowers yellow, red, brown, and blue; Nutmeg burner; 10 inches high. Found also in red satin glass. See Fig. 302. *Bates collection.*

Fig. 304. Milk glass with blue ground top of base and shade; blue flowers with enamel centers; brass pedestal base; P. & A. Victor burner; 11¾ inches high. *Authors' collection.*

Fig. 305. Gold gilted pedestal base; milk glass painted greenish yellow to resemble satin; variegated flowers trimmed in gold; Acorn burner; 11¾ inches high. *Zies collection.*

Fig. 306. Three-tier banquet lamp; brass pedestal base; milk glass with fired-on white flowers and green leaves; P. & A. Victor burner; 17 inches high. *Authors' collection.*

Fig. 307. Milk glass with embossed design; Nutmeg burner; 13 inches high. *Schafer collection.*

141

Fig. 308. Milk glass, painted yellow around top of shade and base; flower decorations in shades of brown and green; Nutmeg burner; 8¾ inches high. *Authors' collection.*

Fig. 309. Milk glass, fired-on pink ground; maps of North and South America with girls holding hands in yellow and red; in gold, "Pan-American Exposition, 1901, Buffalo, N.Y. U.S.A."; Nutmeg burner; 9 inches high. Found also in blue, and in green in a glass textured like an orange skin. *Authors' collection.*

Fig. 310. Green milk glass in a ribbed panel pattern; Nutmeg burner; 8 inches high. Also found in painted milk glass with floral decorations. See Fig. 311. *Authors' collection.*

Fig. 311. Milk glass in a ribbed panel pattern; painted orange ground with flowers in white, red, and yellow; Nutmeg burner; 8 inches high. See Fig. 310. *Funderwhite collection.*

Fig. 312. Milk glass with leaves in brown, green, and yellow on a pink ground; Nutmeg burner; 7½ inches high. *Authors' collection.*

Fig. 313. Milk glass with reddish pink ground and colorful pansies; Nutmeg burner; 8¾ inches high. Also found with several other gay floral patterns. *Authors' collection.*

143

Fig. 314. Milk glass, orange ground fading to yellow, blue flowers and green leaves in fired-on paint; Nutmeg burner; 8¾ inches high. *Lindemuth collection.*

Fig. 315. Milk glass painted blue around top of shade and base, blue and green floral decorations; Nutmeg burner; 8¼ inches high. *Authors' collection.*

Fig. 316. Milk glass painted with shadings of purple around top of shade and base; fired-on flowers in deep wine, leaves green; Nutmeg burner; 8½ inches high. *Authors' collection.*

144

Fig. 317. Milk glass, with bands of fired-on pink paint around base and shade with white flowers with yellow centers; Nutmeg burner; 8½ inches high. Found also with green bands and white flowers. *Authors' collection.*

Fig. 318. Milk glass; fired-on soft cream ground with orange and white flowers; Nutmeg burner; 9 inches high. *Luckenbill collection.*

Fig. 319. Milk glass with painted pale green and pink ground, with red roses and green leaves; Nutmeg burner; 9 inches high. *Bankert collection.*

Fig. 320. Milk glass; pink around top of base and shade, roses pink, leaves green; Nutmeg burner; 8 inches high. Found also with other painted decorations. See Figs. 321 and 322. *Myers collection.*

Fig. 321. Milk glass with fired-on pale pink ground; painted decorations of angels in pink and white; Nutmeg burner; 7¾ inches high. *Authors' collection.*

Fig. 322. Milk glass; white shading to pink, children in blue nightgowns with candles; clear bead fringe; Nutmeg burner; 7½ inches high. *Plasterer collection.*

146

Fig. 323. Prayer lamp; milk glass with fired-on paintings in pink, blue, and green; praying child and clouds on shade, angel and clouds on base; Nutmeg burner; 9 inches high. Found also with paintings in purple. *Authors' collection.*

Fig. 324. Milk glass painted blue to resemble satin glass; angel and decorations in brown; P. & A. Victor burner; 10½ inches high. *Bates collection.*

Fig. 325. Milk glass base with embossed design and angel and other decoration painted in brown, red, and green; clear glass chimney-shade partly frosted, with angel and other decoration matching the base; Hornet burner; 9 inches high. *Authors' collection.*

147

Fig. 326. Peg lamp with matching candlestick; pressed milk glass candlestick with painted brown flowers and green leaves; lamp base painted beige, with angels and flowers in shades of brown; shade beige with top and bottom in clear glass, angels and flowers painted to match base; Hornet burner; 14½ inches high over-all. *Authors' collection.*

Fig. 327. White Bristol-type glass; pictures of children in wheat field in yellow, blue, pink, green, and light brown; Hornet burner; 8¼ inches high. *Authors' collection.*

Fig. 328. Pink milk glass with fired-on angels and other decorations in orange, blue, yellow, and green; foreign burner; 8¾ inches high. *Authors' collection.*

148

Fig. 329. Milk glass with ground pink shading to white; embossed decorations in gold with painted flowers and ferns framing pictures of children and dog scenes in blue, browns, and greens; paint well fired on; foreign burner; 11 inches high. *Funderwhite collection.*

Fig. 330. Milk glass, paneled and embossed; fired-on ground yellow and white with pink and yellow flowers ornamented with gold; foreign burner; 11¾ inches high. *Authors' collection.*

Fig. 331. Milk glass with embossed design; house and windmill scenes painted in shade of blue and green trimmed in gold; on bottom "Amsterdam"; foreign burner; 11¼ inches high. *Authors' collection.*

Fig. 332. Bristol-type milk glass with clear applied feet; windmill and boat scenes painted in shades of blue; Nutmeg burner; 9 inches high. *Authors' collection.*

Fig. 333. Milk glass with painted blue windmill scenes; Nutmeg burner; 7½ inches high. *Luckenbill collection.*

Fig. 334. Milk glass with painted windmill scenes in blues and gray; Hornet burner; 10¼ inches high. *Authors' collection.*

Fig. 335. Porcelain base and milk glass shade, both with painted red roses and green leaves; both have pictures of "Hof-u National Theater Munchen" on one side; on other side of shade is a building "Frauen-kirche Munchen" and on the base a different view of the same; Kosmos-Brenner burner; 10¼ inches high. *Authors' collection.*

Fig. 336. Bristol glass; cream color with brown bands around top and bottom of base and bottom of shade; water scenes of boats and birds in shades of brown; foreign burner; 9 inches high. *Reinert collection.*

Fig. 337. Milk glass; ground beige, with farm scene in various colors; metal around top and bottom of font; Nutmeg burner; 9½ inches high. *Funderwhite collection.*

Fig. 338. Milk glass; base has boat scene painted in various shades of blue; plain Bristol shade; foreign burner; 6 inches high. *Rodney collection.*

Fig. 339. Bristol-type milk glass with green and gray painted scenes; Acorn burner; 7½ inches high. Also found with other scenes in brown. *Authors' collection.*

Fig. 340. Milk glass; fired-on flowers in orange with green leaves; foreign burner; 7½ inches high. *Authors' collection.*

152

Fig. 341. Milk glass decorated with red strawberries, blue flowers, green leaves, and gold bands; foreign burner; 9 inches high. *Bartol collection.*

Fig. 342. Milk glass with roses and other flowers in blue, purple, orange, and pink; paint not well fired on; foreign burner; 8½ inches high. *Ritter collection.*

Fig. 343. Milk glass with flowers in blue, pink, and green; Hornet burner; 10½ inches high. *Reinert collection.*

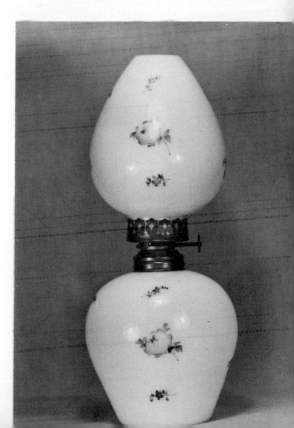

153

Fig. 344. Milk glass painted pink; flowers and other decorations in blue, green, and other colors; foreign burner; 8¾ inches high. *Authors' collection.*

Fig. 345. Triangular shaped lamp in satin milk glass; embossed pink roses and green and yellow leaves; foreign burner; 9 inches high. Found also in frosted clear glass. *Authors' collection.*

Fig. 346. Pink milk glass; fired-on birds in yellow, orange, and brown; flower sprays in yellow, blue, green, and brown; foreign burner; 8½ inches high. Found also in blue milk glass with the same decorations. *Authors' collection.*

154

Fig. 347. Milk glass; fired-on paint designs in green, yellow, and tan; applied handle; foreign burner; 8 inches high. *Funderwhite collection.*

Fig. 348. Brass base and font; milk glass with painted grayish tan ground with owl in natural colors; paint fired on; Nutmeg burner; 9¼ inches high. *Wehle collection.*

Fig. 349. Milk glass; ground painted greenish yellow with pink bands; foreign lamp with a Nutmeg burner; 9½ inches high. *Zies collection.*

Fig. 350. Blue milk glass; enameled flowers in brown, white, green, and blue; foreign burner; 7½ inches high. *Ritter collection.*

Fig. 351. Milk glass with fired-on green ground, red flowers, green leaves, and gold bands; foreign burner; 8½ inches high. *Authors' collection.*

Fig. 352. Embossed milk glass, dark green shading to light green ground; flowers pink; gold decorations; foreign burner; 9 inches high. *Authors' collection.*

Fig. 359. Pea-green milk glass w...
buff coralene flowers; painted gr...
leaves and other decorations...
orange and gold; foreign bur...
9¾ inches high. *Authors' collec...*

Fig. 353. Milk glass; floral decorations in yellow, blue, white, and green on an orange ground; paint fired on; foreign burner; 9¼ inches high. *Wehle collection.*

Fig. 360. Milk glass trimmed in...
ious shades of blue with flowe...
blue, red, and orange well fired...
foreign burner; 9½ inches...
Ritter collection.

Fig. 354. Milk glass, painted orchid shading to purple; floral decorations in enamel are white and purple; foreign burner; 9½ inches high. *Authors' collection.*

Fig. 361. Blue milk glass; fl...
enameled in white, red, yellow...
ange, and green, narrow pa...
red bands; foreign burner; 9 i...
high. *Funderwhite collection.*

Fig. 355. Milk glass decorated with orange figures, flowers in blue with green leaves and stems; foreign burner; 9¼ inches high. *Authors' collection.*

159

157

Fig. 362. Bristol-type milk glass; fired-on floral decorations in orange, blue, and green; foreign burner; 7 inches high. *Authors' collection.*

Fig. 363. Milk glass with enameled flowers in orange and blue with green leaves; narrow gold bands around base and shade; clear glass prisms; foreign burner; 9½ inches high. *Authors' collection.*

Fig. 364. White satin glass; painted flowers in orchid, yellow, and green; crystal prisms; Nutmeg burner; 6 inches high. There is some question of the authenticity of this lamp. *Authors' collection.*

Fig. 365. Blue milk glass with embossed square base and gold decorations; "Gute Nacht" in gold on shade; foreign burner, probably German; 6½ inches high. *Authors' collection.*

Fig. 366. Milk glass; embossed sawtooth and ribbon; foreign burner; 6½ inches high. Found also in clear and in green glass. *Authors' collection.*

Fig. 367. Beaded ribbed End-of-Day overlay in brown, red, green, and blue with yellow lining; Hornet burner; 9 inches high. *Bartol collection.*

Fig. 368. Mottled brown, pink, and green glass (Tortoise-shell) cased over white glass with a molded beaded rib pattern; Hornet burner; 9 inches high. *Wehle collection.*

Fig. 369. Embossed beaded swirl pattern in brown, red, and yellow End-of-Day glass; Hornet burner; 8¾ inches high. Found also in cased glass in yellow and red End-of-Day and in olive-green, crystal, cranberry, amethyst, and milk glass. *Authors' collection.*

Fig. 370. Embossed beaded swirl, iridescent cranberry glass with grayish overshot; Hornet burner; 8¾ inches high. *Authors' collection.*

162

Fig. 371. Embossed beaded swirl; clear glass gilted in bronze and gold, not fired on and partly worn off; Hornet burner; 8½ inches high. *Authors' collection.*

Fig. 372. Cased glass, butterscotch with custard lining; embossed flowers and design; Hornet burner; 8 inches high. *Bates collection.*

Fig. 373. Custard glass, embossed flowers and design; Hornet burner; 8¼ inches high. *Wehle collection.*

163

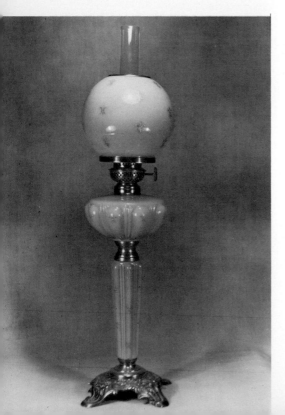

Fig. 374. Pink cased glass with embossed design; Hornet burner; 8¾ inches high. Found also in milk glass with green trim and blue and orchid flowers and also with pink trim and similar flowers. *Authors' collection.*

Fig. 375. Pale pink shading to apricot cased glass with embossed design; foreign burner; 10½ inches high. Also found in blue and deep rose both shading to white. *Authors' collection.*

Fig. 376. Three-tier banquet lamp; brass pedestal base; pink overlay with gold enameled fleur-de-lis; P. & A. Victor burner; 16½ inches high. *Authors' collection.*

Fig. 377. Cased glass, pink shading to delicate pink, white lining; applied clear glass shell feet; "Prima-Rund-Brenner" burner; 12 inches high. *Authors' collection.*

Fig. 378. Red cased glass with white lining; white enameled flowers and fruit; gold decorations; made-up burner; 11 inches high. *Funderwhite collection.*

Fig. 379. Yellow cased glass with embossed pattern; Nutmeg burner; 8½ inches high. Found also in pink cased glass. *Authors' collection.*

Fig. 380. White satin glass painted orchid around top of base and shade; floral sprays in blue, yellow, and brown; Nutmeg burner; 7 inches high. Made by Consolidated Lamp and Glass Co., Pittsburgh, Pa., about 1894. *Bartol collection.*

Fig. 381. Pink satin glass with base encased in silver filigree; Nutmeg burner; 7 inches high. Made by Consolidated Lamp and Glass Co., Pittsburgh, Pa., about 1894. *Authors' collection.*

Fig. 382. Pink cased glass; embossed design; foreign burner; 8 inches high. *Authors' collection.*

Fig. 383. "Acme" night lamp; green milk glass; Nutmeg burner; 6½ inches high. Found also in rose and in yellow. Made by Westmoreland Specialty Co., Grapeville, Pa., and called "Acme" in their catalog of 1890. See Fig. 389. *Authors' collection.*

Fig. 384. Pink cased glass in glossy finish; Nutmeg burner; 6½ inches high. Found also in aqua blue. This base is identical in shape to "Acme" (Fig. 383) while the shade is identical in shape to Fig. 385. Since we have seen three lamps in two colors we believe this combination to be original. *Authors' collection.*

Fig. 385. Pink cased glass with satin finish; Nutmeg burner; 7 inches high. Found also in blue, white, pink, yellow, and light peach cased glass in glossy finish. Some of the various shades of pink are mottled with white and are erroneously called "pink slag." These lamps are also found in satin glass with various painted floral decorations and with silver filigree. See Figs. 380 and 381, and color Fig. V. Made by Consolidated Lamp and Glass Co., Pittsburgh, Pa., about 1894. *Authors' collection.*

167

Fig. 392. White satin glass with embossed hearts and scrolls, painted in gold; Hornet-type burner; 8 inches high. *Authors' collection.*

Fig. 393. White satin glass with embossed ribbing; fired-on paint in pink, yellow, and green; Nutmeg burner; 7½ inches high. *Authors' collection.*

Fig. 394. Pink cased satin glass in a diamond puffed pattern; Nutmeg burner; 8 inches high. Found also in green, yellow, and light blue in satin finish and in pink and yellow cased with crystal. Made by Consolidated Lamp and Glass Co., Pittsburgh, Pa., about 1894. *Authors' collection.*

Fig. 395. Blue satin glass with embossed floral design; Nutmeg burner; 7½ inches high. Also found in rose color. In C. M. Linnington's catalog, "Silent Salesman," of Jan. 1894 it is called "Idaho Night Lamp" and priced at $4.35 per dozen. *Luckenbill collection.*

Fig. 396. Blue satin glass with beaded panels with embossed scrolls and flowers; Nutmeg burner; 7¾ inches high. Also found in milk glass with flowers painted red and green. *Plasterer collection.*

Fig. 397. Red satin glass with embossed design; Nutmeg burner; 8¼ inches high. *Authors' collection.*

Fig. 398. Red satin glass with embossed Plume pattern; Nutmeg burner; 8¾ inches high. *Sullivan collection.*

Fig. 399. Red satin glass with textured surface and embossed beaded panels and decorations; Nutmeg burner; 7¾ inches high. Found also in orange satin glass and in blue satin glass. *Authors' collection.*

Fig. 400. Red satin glass with beaded Drape pattern; Nutmeg burner; 9 inches high. Also found in blue, green, and pink satin glass and in glossy white opalescent with ruby thumbprints. It is currently made in all these colors in satin and possibly others. See Fig. 403. *Authors' collection.*

172

Fig. 401. Red satin glass with embossed design; Nutmeg burner; 7¾ inches high. *Authors' collection.*

Fig. 402. Blue glass with satin finish and embossed design; foreign burner; 9 inches high. *Authors' collection.*

Fig. 403. Beaded Drape pattern in white opalescent with ruby thumbprints; Nutmeg burner; 9½ inches high. See Fig. 400. *Clark collection.*

Fig. 404. Pink opaline glass with enamel flowers and leaves; foreign burner; 9½ inches high. *Authors' collection.*

Fig. 405. Red satin glass; Hornet burner; 9½ inches high. *Bartol collection.*

Fig. 406. Satin milk glass with embossed design; floral decorations in yellow and green are badly worn; Spar-Brenner burner; 8¾ inches high. *Authors' collection.*

174

Fig. 407. White opaline glass with embossed design; foreign burner; 8½ inches high. *Bartol collection.*

Fig. 408. Blue opaline glass with embossed ribbing, flowers, and leaves; foreign burner; 8¼ inches high. Found also in pink opaline. *Authors' collection.*

Fig. 409. Blue opaline glass with embossed design; foreign burner; 8¾ inches high. Found also in pink and in white. *Authors' collection.*

175

Fig. 410. Pink opaline glass with embossed design; foreign burner; 7 inches high. Found also in blue opaline glass. *Authors' collection.*

Fig. 411. Base overshot; purple glass band around top of base and top of shade; enameled flowers and house in purple and white; clear applied handle; foreign burner; 7 inches high. *Schafer collection.*

Fig. 412. Cranberry glass lamp and chimney; Mary Gregory-type white enamel painting of girl with net catching butterflies; foreign burner; 9 inches high. *Authors' collection.*

176

Fig. 413. Clear glass, white over-shot appearance; reddish brown house and green trees; on reverse side, a winter scene with snow on trees; foreign burner; 7 inches high. *Myers collection.*

Fig. 414. Overshot glass, clear shading to green; foreign burner; 7 inches high. *Reinert collection.*

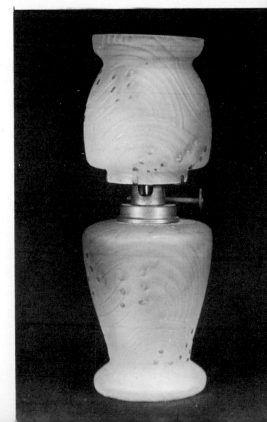

Fig. 415. Frosted glass with a swirl design; embossed gold dots; foreign burner; 7½ inches high. *Luckenbill collection.*

Fig. 416. Frosted clear glass; decorations and flowers in gold; foreign burner; 7¼ inches high. *Wehle collection.*

Fig. 417. Rainbow glass in ribbed pattern with a glossy finish; foreign burner; 6¾ inches high. *Authors' collection.*

Fig. 418. Clear glass painted green to resemble satin; foreign burner; 6¾ inches high. *Wehle collection.*

Fig. 419. White with rainbow luster finish; embossed design; Nutmeg burner; 7¾ inches high. We believe this lamp to be old, but this pattern is reproduced in several colors. *Agnew collection.*

Fig. 420. Frosted glass with enamel decorations in yellow, blue, and orange; foreign burner; 7½ inches high. *Bartol collection.*

Fig. 421. Iridescent pale pink glass in a ribbed swirl pattern; foreign burner; 6½ inches high. *Authors' collection.*

Fig. 422. White iridescent textured glass; enameled floral decorations in blue, white, and green; foreign burner; 6½ inches high. *Bates collection.*

Fig. 423. Iridescent red glass with embossed pattern; Nutmeg burner; 9 inches high. Found also in honey color. *Authors' collection.*

Fig. 424. Brown iridescent with golden brown frill around top of shade; enameled lilies of the valley in white with green leaves; foreign burner; 8 inches high. *Bates collection.*

Fig. 425. Iridescent green glass with embossed decorations; Nutmeg burner; 10 inches high. *Authors' collection.*

Fig. 426. Clear glass painted pale blue to resemble satin; enameled white flowers, green leaves, blue berries, and gold bands; foreign burner; 9½ inches high. *Authors' collection.*

Fig. 427. Clear glass painted to resemble iridescent; enameled butterflies and flowers in blue, green, yellow, and brown; foreign burner; 9 inches high. *Bates collection.*

Fig. 428. White overshot glass with art nouveau decorations in gold, green, and orange enamel; foreign burner; 9½ inches high. *Bartol collection.*

Fig. 429. White overshot; flowers and leaves painted with blue, green, and orange transparent stain and are not overshot; foreign burner; 7 inches high. *Zies collection.*

Fig. 430. Clear glass with almost clear satin finish painted on; painted red strawberries and green leaves; foreign burner; 9 inches high. *Authors' collection.*

Fig. 431. Rubina crystal in Ivy pattern with embossed ivy and swirl; the ivy is glossy finish, the rest is satin; Nutmeg burner; 6½ inches high. Found also in cranberry and in crystal. *Authors' collection.*

Fig. 432. "Twinkle" lamp; blue glass with embossed name "Twinkle" and stars on base and stars on shade; Acorn burner; 7 inches high. Found also in amethyst, green, and amber glass. *Authors' collection.*

Fig. 433. Blue glass in Honeycomb pattern; Nutmeg burner; 6¾ inches high. *Bartol collection.*

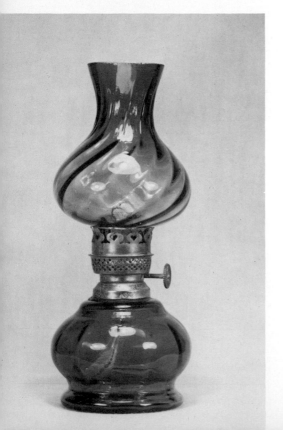

Fig. 434. Cranberry glass in Inverted Thumbprint pattern; Nutmeg burner; 8 inches high. *Ritter collection.*

Fig. 435. Green glass with a faintly paneled swirl pattern; foreign burner; 7½ inches high. *Sullivan collection.*

Fig. 436. Green glass with faintly paneled swirl shade and faintly paneled base; foreign burner; 7½ inches high. *Bartol collection.*

184

Fig. 437. Cranberry glass, paneled base; Hornet burner 9½ inches high. *Wehle collection.*

Fig. 438. Cranberry glass, hexagonal base, paneled shade; foreign burner; 9½ inches high. *Lindemuth collection.*

Fig. 439. Amberina glass; Hornet burner; 8¼ inches high. Found also in cranberry, opalescent, light green, and vaseline. *Authors' collection.*

185

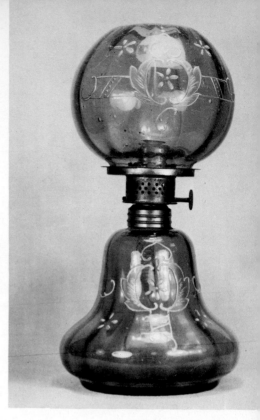

Fig. 440. Amberina glass; Nutmeg burner; 9 inches high. *Bates collection.*

Fig. 441. Cranberry glass, faintly ribbed; fired-on decorations in gold; Nutmeg burner; 8¾ inches high. *Wehle collection.*

Fig. 442. Cranberry glass, shade faintly paneled; Hornet burner; 9½ inches high. *Bartol collection.*

Fig. 443. Cranberry glass with embossed design; foreign burner; 8½ inches high. *Lindemuth collection.*

Fig. 444. Cranberry glass with enameled white flowers; Nutmeg burner; 8½ inches high. *Authors' collection.*

Fig. 445. Amber glass with embossed scrolls; Hornet burner; 8½ inches high. Made about 1899 by Eagle Glass & Mfg. Co., Wellsburg, W. Va. In Montgomery Ward & Co. catalog for 1901 it is pictured for 30¢ each. *Authors' collection.*

187

Fig. 446. Blue glass with embossed swirls and flowers; flowers in white enamel; foreign burner; 9½ inches high. *Bates collection.*

Fig. 447. Blue glass; enameled decorations of pink and white flowers and yellow dots; foreign burner; 8½ inches high. *Bartol collection.*

Fig. 448. Amber glass with embossed ribbing around top of shade; decorations and flowers in blue and white; unusual burner with no mark; 10 inches high. *Schafer collection.*

Fig. 449. Green glass; base has embossed ribs around bottom and top and embossed flowers; shade has indistinct panels; gold gilt trim badly worn; Hornet burner; 8¾ inches high. Found also in blue and in milk glass. *Authors' collection.*

Fig. 450. Green glass with enameled white flowers; Hornet burner; 8¼ inches high. *Authors' collection.*

Fig. 451. Amber glass with enameled flowers and leaves in blue and white; Hornet burner; 7½ inches high. *Ritter collection.*

189

Fig. 452. Green glass with white flowers partly worn off; Acorn burner; 6¾ inches high. *Authors' collection.*

Fig. 453. Amber glass with glossy finish and embossed design; foreign burner; 7½ inches high. *Luckenbill collection.*

Fig. 454. Green glass with geometric decoration in gold outlined with white enamel, and gold bands; foreign burner; 7¼ inches high. *Wehle collection.*

Fig. 455. Green porcelain with raised design; foreign burner; 7 inches high. *Bates collection.*

Fig. 456. Green glass with flowers and bands in gold, partly worn off; Hornet burner; 9 inches high. *Bartol collection.*

Fig. 457. Green glass with floral sprays of pink, white, yellow, and green enamel and gold bands; foreign burner; 7½ inches high. *Bartol collection.*

Fig. 458. Blue glass decorated in gold with enameled leaves and berries in white; Hornet burner; 11 inches high. *Funderwhite collection.*

Fig. 459. Cranberry glass with white enamel flowers and leaves; foreign burner; 9¾ inches high. *Authors' collection.*

Fig. 460. Cranberry glass with white enamel decorations; foreign burner; 9¾ inches high. *Authors' collection.*

Fig. 461. Cranberry glass; applied clear glass feet; jack-in-the-pulpit shade; foreign burner; 9¾ inches to highest point. *Authors' collection.*

Fig. 462. Cranberry glass with embossed base and ribbed shade; foreign burner; 9½ inches high. *Authors' collection.*

Fig. 463. Lighthouse lamp of blue transparent glass; foreign burner; 7 inches high. *Bartol collection.*

Fig. 464. Blue glass with embossed design; foreign burner; 9 inches high. *Authors' collection.*

Fig. 465. Cranberry glass with embossed design; Hornet burner; 8 inches high. *Bates collection.*

Fig. 466. Green glass in Diamond pattern; foreign burner; 9 inches high. *Bartol collection.*

194

Fig. 467. Embossed blue glass with gold decorations; Acorn burner; 6½ inches high. *Authors' collection.*

Fig. 468. Green glass with swirl design; foreign burner; 8 inches high. *Bartol collection.*

Fig. 469. Green glass faintly paneled; enameled flowers in brown, yellow, white, and gold; Nutmeg burner; 8 inches high. *Bates collection.*

Fig. 470. Green glass with enameled flowers in white and orange and gold decorations; shade faintly paneled; Nutmeg burner; 7¼ inches high. *Authors' collection.*

Fig. 471. Blue Spanish lace lamp; Nutmeg burner; 7¾ inches high. Found also in cranberry and in vaseline. *Authors' collection.*

Fig. 472. Blue glass with white enamel dots and flowers and narrow gold bands; foreign burner; 5½ inches high. *Bartol collection.*

Fig. 473. Blue Spanish lace lamp covered with silver filigree; Nutmeg burner; 7 inches high. See Fig. 474. *Plasterer collection.*

Fig. 474. Reddish purple Spanish lace lamp encased in silver filigree; Nutmeg burner; 7 inches high. Found also in blue Spanish lace both with and without filigree. See Fig. 473. *Authors' collection.*

Fig. 475. Blue glass with a swirl pattern; Nutmeg burner; 9 inches high. *Authors' collection.*

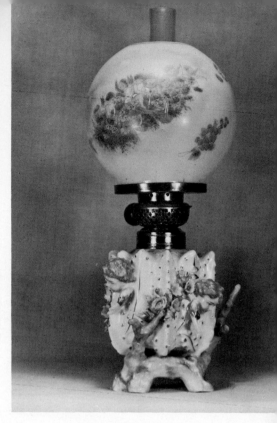

Fig. 482. Embossed Daisy and Cube pattern in blue glass; Nutmeg burner; 8 inches high. Found also in amber, crystal, and vaseline. A very similar lamp is extensively reproduced at the present time in several colors. It can be identified by the font, which is more apple shaped, and by the shade, which is higher. *Authors' collection.*

Fig. 483. Dresden base decorated in gold and beige; Bristol shade with floral decorations in various colors; foreign burner; 10¾ inches high. *Funderwhite collection.*

Fig. 484. Porcelain House lamp; embossed green trim and multi-colored flowers; foreign burner; 7½ inches high. *Authors' collection.*

200

Fig. 485. Bisque boy with cart, painted in dark ivory, blue, pink, brown, and other colors; wicker shade with cloth lining of dark ivory; Acorn burner; 9 inches high. *Authors' collection.*

Fig. 486. Jasper ware; green base with white boy; Bristol-type white shade with embossed design; foreign burner; 6½ inches high. *Authors' collection.*

Fig. 487. Porcelain man and barrel lamp in brown and yellow; English burner; 3½ inches high. *Authors' collection.*

201

Fig. 488. Reclining Elephant lamp; milk glass; base is reclining elephant, shade is ribbed swirl with acanthus leaf decorations; the orange, yellow, and gold paint is badly worn; Nutmeg burner; 7¾ inches high. In Butler Brothers' catalog "Our Drummer" for Feb. 1900 this lamp is pictured and described: "Lamp represents an elephant kneeling, caparison and houdah painted in rich colors and gold." Price $2.25 per dozen. (This same shade pattern is used on the Acanthus lamp. See Fig. 232. On the elephant lamp it measures 3 inches in diameter and 3 inches high; on the Acanthus lamp, 4 inches in diameter and 3 inches high.) Authors' collection.

Fig. 489. Bisque girl and boy, painted in beige, green, yellow, and gold; frosted glass shades with designs in brown and white; foreign burners; 8¾ inches high. Bartol collection.

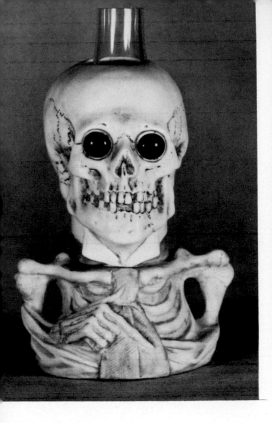

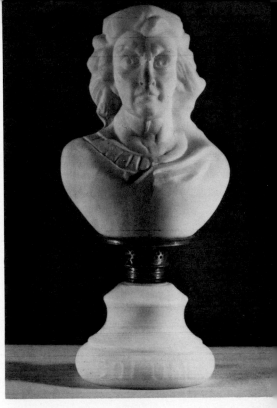

Fig. 490. Skeleton lamp; white bisque, blue and orchid trim; green glass eyes; foreign burner, possibly German; 5½ inches high. Found also in a larger size, 6¾ inches high. *Authors' collection.*

Fig. 491. Columbus lamp; milk glass with "Columbus" embossed on base; rough satin finish; Nutmeg burner; 10 inches high. Found also in glossy finish milk glass. Made by Consolidated Lamp and Glass Co., Pittsurgh, Pa., about 1894. *Authors' collection.*

Fig. 492. Reclining Camel lamp; base in white and blue porcelain; white Bristol shade; foreign burner; 6 inches to top of shade. *Plasterer collection.*

203

Fig. 493. Embossed clear glass; embossed owl face on one side of shade; Nutmeg burner; 8 inches high. Found also in green milk glass. *Wehle collection.*

Fig. 494. Bulldog lamp; clear frosted glass with gilt decorations; Hornet burner; 8 inches high. We have also seen a green satin glass base. *Authors' collection.*

Fig. 495. Bisque Owl lamp in various shades of brown and yellow; brown glass eyes; foreign burner; 7½ inches high. This lamp was made for oil, but we have seen one just like it made for burning short candles. *Bartol collection.*

204

Fig. 496. Porcelain Cat lamp; white cat with yellowish green glass cat eyes; green base; orange ball; Hornet-size burner; 6 inches high. *Lindemuth collection.*

Fig. 497. Owl lamp; milk glass with fired-on paint in black and grays with orange eyes; the shade has a face on both sides; Nutmeg burner; 7¾ inches high. Found also painted in dark and light green and in different shades of reddish brown. *Authors' collection.*

Fig. 498. Porcelain Turtle lamp in green, brown, and yellow; white shade; foreign burner; 5¼ inches high. *Wehle collection.*

205

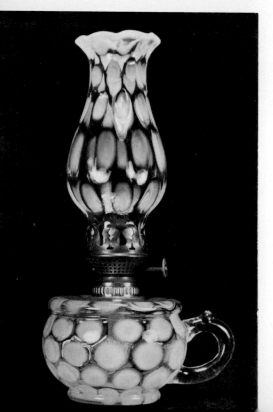

Fig. 505. Threaded glass lamp; greenish glass threaded with red; foreign burner; 10 inches high. *Authors' collection.*

Fig. 506. Green opalescent glass in Hobnail pattern; Hornet burner; 8½ inches high. *Wehle collection.*

Fig. 507. Crystal with opalescent white Thumbprint pattern; applied crystal handle; Falk's burner (English); 10½ inches high. *Ritter collection.*

208

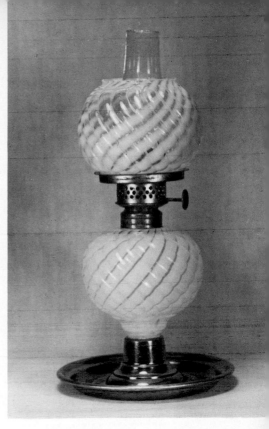

Fig. 508. White opalescent Spanish lace; clear pedestal base; Nutmeg burner; 8 inches high. *Plasterer collection.*

Fig. 509. White opalescent and clear glass swirls; brass saucer base; Nutmeg burner; 6½ inches high. Also found in blue and in pink with clear swirls. *Bates collection.*

Fig. 510. White opalescent glass with blue "eyes"; clear pedestal base; Nutmeg burner; 7½ inches high. Found also with pink and with red "eyes" on white opalescent ground. *Bartol collection.*

209

Fig. 511. Cranberry glass with white opalescent stripes; foreign burner; 9¼ inches high. *Luckenbill collection.*

Fig. 512. Clear glass with opal swirl; Nutmeg burner; 6½ inches high. Found also in vaseline with opal swirl. *Authors' collection.*

Fig. 513. Cranberry and white glass in a swirl pattern; clear glass pedestal base; Nutmeg burner; 8 inches high. Found also in blue and white swirl. *Authors' collection.*

210

Fig. 514. Yellow opalescent swirl pattern; clear applied feet; foreign burner; 7½ inches high. Found also in red swirl. *Luckenbill collection.*

Fig. 515. Opal, pink, and clear glass stripes; clear applied feet; matching shade and chimney; Nutmeg burner; 7½ inches high. *Authors' collection.*

Fig. 516. Red glass with white opalescent stripes; Acorn burner; 8 inches high. *Bates collection.*

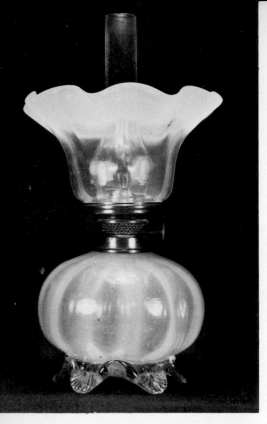

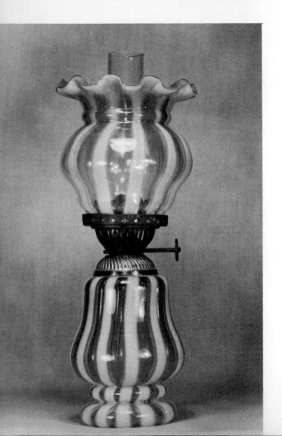

Fig. 517. White opalescent glass; applied blue shell feet; foreign burner; 7¼ inches high. *Agnew collection.*

Fig. 518. Vaseline glass with opalescent Thumbprint pattern; foreign burner; 9 inches high. *Plasterer collection.*

Fig. 519. Cranberry glass with white opalescent stripes; foreign burner; 9½ inches high. *Funderwhite collection.*

212

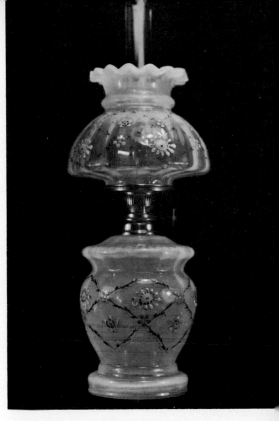

Fig. 520. Vaseline opalescent with relief design of flowers and leaves; foreign burner; 8½ inches high. *Wehle collection.*

Fig. 521. Opalescent pale blue glass with enameled flowers in pink, orange, white, brown, and gold; foreign burner; 9¼ inches high. *Authors' collection.*

Fig. 522. Vertical ribbed pale pink opalescent; applied opalescent flower on base; opalescent chimney to match; applied green shells around top of base and as feet; foreign burner; 10½ inches high. *Schafer collection.*

213

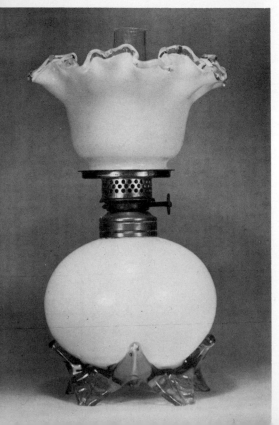

Fig. 523. Blue opalescent; applied red trim around top of shade; applied clear glass feet; matching chimney; foreign burner; 7¾ inches high. *Wehle collection.*

Fig. 524. Blue opalescent; matching chimney; clear glass applied feet; foreign burner; 7 inches high. *Wehle collection.*

Fig. 525. Milk glass; amber around top of shade and amber applied feet; Nutmeg burner; 8 inches high. *Wehle collection.*

Fig. 526. Cranberry glass; matching cranberry chimney; clear glass shell applied feet; foreign burner; 7½ inches high. *Wehle collection.*

Fig. 527. Cranberry glass in Diamond pattern; applied clear glass feet; Nutmeg burner; 8 inches high. *Bates collection.*

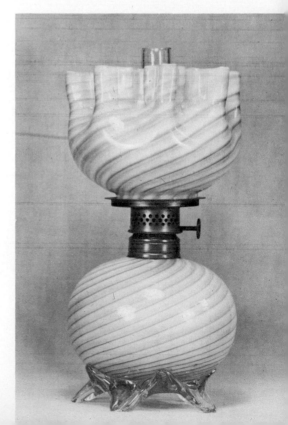

Fig. 528. Candy-stripe pink and white cased glass; applied clear glass feet; Nutmeg burner; 8 inches high. *Lindemuth collection.*

215

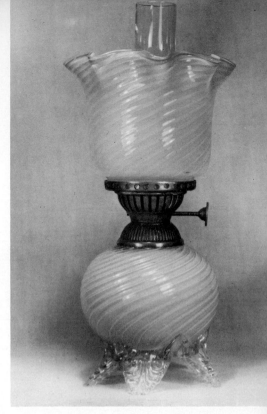

Fig. 529. Candy-stripe pink and white cased glass with white lining; applied crystal feet; Hornet-sized burner; 8 inches high. *Authors' collection.*

Fig. 530. Pink cased glass with white lining; Ribbed Swirl pattern; clear glass applied shell feet; foreign burner; 8 inches high. *Bates collection.*

Fig. 531. White cut velvet, Diamond pattern; applied blue satin feet; Nutmeg burner; 7¾ inches high. Found also in yellow and in blue. *Schafer collection.*

Fig. 532. White satin glass; Ribbed Swirl pattern; applied frosted feet; foreign burner; 8¼ inches high. Ritter collection.

Fig. 533. Yellow satin cut velvet, Diamond pattern; applied frosted ruffle around bottom of base; Nutmeg burner; 6¾ inches high. Found also in blue. Authors' collection.

Fig. 534. Blue cut velvet, Diamond pattern; Nutmeg burner; 7 inches high. Wehle collection.

217

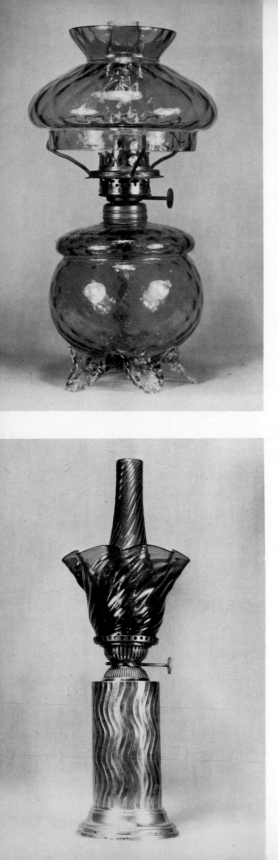

Fig. 535. Cranberry glass, Diamond pattern; applied clear glass feet; Nutmeg burner; 8½ inches high. *Agnew collection.*

Fig. 536. Cranberry glass with applied clear glass shell feet ornaments about the bottom of base; Nutmeg burner; 8¾ inches high. Also found in amber glass. *Authors' collection.*

Fig. 537. Sterling silver, swirl embossed base ;cranberry swirl shade and matching chimney; foreign burner; 10 inches high. *Wehle collection.*

218

Fig. 538. Amberina with applied amber glass feet and ornaments at bottom of base; Nutmeg burner; 8 inches high. Found also In pink opalescent and in pinkish green opalescent both with applied green glass feet and ornaments. *Authors' collection.*

Fig. 539. Ribbed swirled opalescent pink glass with green applied feet and ornaments at bottom of base; Nutmeg burner; 8 inches high. Also found in apricot glass in satin finish with applied clear glass frosted feet and ornaments on base. *Authors' collection.*

Fig. 540. Cranberry glass fading to clear glass; embossed swirl; foreign burner; 7½ inches high. *Bartol collection.*

219

Fig. 541. Raspberry satin glass; Ribbed Swirl pattern on diamond-shaped base and umbrella shade; Nutmeg burner; 8 inches high. *Schafer collection.*

Fig. 542. Cased glass, yellow over white; diamond-shaped base; embossed swirls and design around top of shade; trimmed in gold not well fired on; Nutmeg burner; 8½ inches high. *Zies collection.*

Fig. 543. Amber and honey swirl with bottom of pedestal in amber; Nutmeg burner; 9 inches high. *Wehle collection.*

Fig. 544. Butterscotch and honey color; swirl and embossed ribbed, swirls run one way and ribs the other; pink glass applied feet; foreign burner; 8½ inches high. *Wehle collection.*

Fig. 545. Ribbed Swirl, cobalt blue with clear applied feet; Nutmeg burner; 8¾ inches high. *Schafer collection.*

Fig. 546. Cranberry glass in Ribbed Swirl with applied clear shell feet and ornamentation at bottom of base; Nutmeg burner; 8 inches high. *Authors' collection.*

Fig. 547. Ribbed swirl with four recessed medallions in shade and base; End-of-Day cased glass in various colors; clear glass applied feet; Nutmeg burner; 8¾ inches high. Also found in yellow cased glass, blue milk glass, and in variegated colors in overshot and crackle glass. *Schafer collection.*

Fig. 548. End-of-Day glass; cased ribbed swirl, yellow, red, and black predominating, with greenish yellow lining; clear glass applied feet; Hornet burner; 9 inches high. *Sullivan collection.*

Fig. 549. End-of-Day ribbed swirl; variegated colors of pink, green, brown, and white; applied clear glass feet; Hornet burner; 8½ inches high. *Plasterer collection.*

Fig. 550. Millefiori satin glass in various colors of canes; foreign burner; 8½ inches high. *Wehle collection.*

Fig. 551. End-of-Day overlay, red, white, blue, green, pink, yellow, and orange; applied clear glass feet; Hornet burner; 9½ inches high. *Luckenbill collection.*

Fig. 552. Milk glass with applied red cherries and amber ornamentation and feet; chimney partly frosted and iridescent; Hornet-type burner; 10¼ inches high. *Authors' collection.*

Fig. 553. Cut overlay lamp; cranberry on amber (possibly Stevens and Williams); foreign burner; 8¾ inches high. *Schafer collection.*

Fig. 554. Gold washed base with removable oil font; shade in satin glass, orange-pink shading to light; Nutmeg burner; 8¼ inches high. *Schafer collection.*

Fig. 555. White glossy glass with splashes of red and flecks of mica; raised design; Nutmeg burner; 6½ inches high. Also found in satin glass in pink and in butterscotch. *Schafer collection.*

Fig. 556. Sterling silver base with engraved leaves and flowers; shade is ribbed swirl with embossed decorations in light red glass; raised swirls are frosted clear glass with enameled blue, green, and white flowers and decorations; on foreign burner is "The Silver Light Co."; 9 inches high. *Authors' collection.*

Fig. 557. Yellow shading to white satin glass; white enamel flower sprays; square base in brass holder; foreign burner; 11 inches high. *Luckenbill collection.*

Fig. 558. Gold plated rooster base; yellow cased glass shade with gold dragon design; foreign burner; 10¼ inches high. *Schafer collection.*

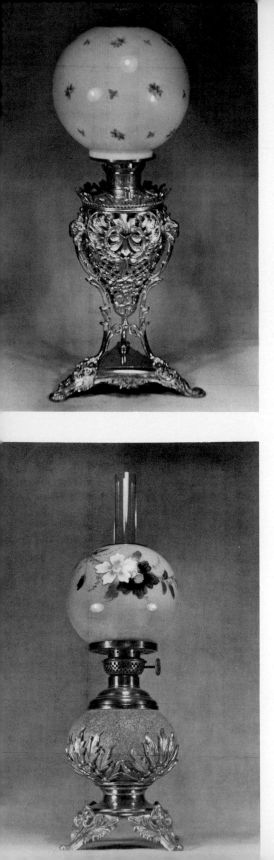

Fig. 559. Brass banquet lamp with removable oil font; milk glass shade with pink and green floral decorations; "B. & H." (Bradley & Hubbard Mfg. Co.) burner; 16¼ inches high. *Authors' collection.*

Fig. 560. Brass saucer base; blue milk glass shading to white; gold decorations and enamel flowers in pink and white; foreign burner; 10¼ inches high. *Wehle collection.*

Fig. 561. Brass base; pottery font with removable oil tank; cased glass shade in orange with enameled flowers in red, white, and gold; P. & A. Victor burner; 12 inches high. *Authors' collection.*

226

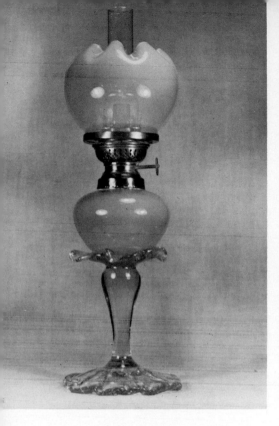

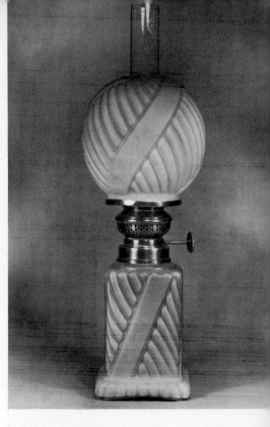

Fig. 562. Green glass pedestal base
with rose opaline font and shade;
foreign burner; 12½ inches high.
Authors' collection.

Fig. 563. Satin glass with swirl pattern; dark rose shading to light;
Kosmos burner, possibly German;
11½ inches high. *Authors' collection.*

Fig. 564. Satin milk glass with embossed shell pattern; painted blue
fading to white; applied frosted
glass feet; Kosmos burner; 10½
inches high. *Bates collection.*

Fig. 565. Satin glass; dark apricot shading to almost white; embossed design; foreign burner; 11¼ inches high. *Ritter collection.*

Fig. 566. Salmon cased glass in Hobnail pattern with applied crystal leaf-shaped feet; foreign burner; 11¼ inches high. *Schafer collection.*

Fig. 567. Pink overshot with clear glass fleur-de-lis; foreign burner; 10 inches high. *Schafer collection.*

228

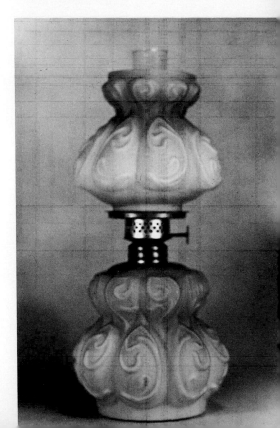

Fig. 568. Embossed satin glass; rose shading to light pink; Nutmeg burner; 9 inches high. Found also in chartreuse. *Luckenbill collection.*

Fig. 569. Chartreuse cased glass with embossed design; foreign burner; 9 inches high. *Bartol collection.*

Fig. 570. Embossed satin glass; white shading to green; Nutmeg burner; 10 inches high. *Luckenbill collection.*

Fig. 571. Signed Crown Milano glass; all-over raised design; floral decorations of brown and blue; foreign burner; 8 inches high. *Schafer collection.*

Fig. 572. Yellow satin glass with fired-on brown leaves and pink enameled flowers; foreign burner; 7½ inches high. *Authors' collection.*

Fig. 573. Satin glass, pink shading to white; embossed design; foreign burner; 9 inches high. *Funderwhite collection.*

Fig. 574. Fireglow glass; melon-ribbed base; enameled design of foliage in rust and brown; foreign burner; 6¼ inches high. *Schafer collection.*

Fig. 575. Orange shading to delicate pink, satin finish; white flowers and green leaves in enamel; foreign burner; 9 inches high. *Authors' collection.*

Fig. 576. Chartreuse Verre Moire (Nailsea) glass lamp set into a matching footed flower-bowl base; foreign burner; 9½ inches high. A lamp of this description was registered at the London Patent Office by Charles Kempton and Sons, wholesale distributors of glass and china, on Nov. 19, 1886. *Schafer collection.*

Fig. 577. Shaded rose Verre Moire (Nailsea) glass with frosted clear glass applied feet and ruffle-edge on base; foreign burner; 9 inches high. *Wehle collection.*

Fig. 578. Rose Verre Moire (Nailsea) glass shade and font on a red velvet cushion; foreign burner; 8¼ inches high. *Schafer collection.*

Fig. 579. Red satin glass in a swirl pattern on a red plush base; foreign burner; 7½ inches high. Found also in blue. *Authors' collection.*

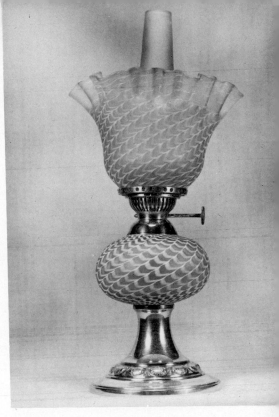

Fig. 580. White and clear **Verre Moire** (Nailsea) glass, satin finish; foreign burner; 10 inches high. *Wehle collection.*

Fig. 581. Blue and white **Verre Moire** (Nailsea) glass with satin finish; silver base and collar; foreign burner; 10 inches high. *Wehle collection.*

Fig. 582. **Verre Moire** (Nailsea) glass in pulled red and beige; brass base; foreign burner; 12½ inches high. *Wehle collection.*

233

Fig. 583. Green satin decorated with silver berries and leaves; Spar-Brenner burner; 14¼ inches high. *Authors' collection.*

Fig. 584. Transparent green glass with gold, blue, pink, and white enamel decorations; marked "Vonicean"; foreign burner; 9¼ inches high. *Wehle collection.*

Fig. 585. Frosted clear glass with enameled flowers in pink, yellow, green, and white, painted on both sides of the glass to give depth; foreign burner; 13¾ inches high. *Authors' collection.*

Fig. 586. Tiffany lamp; greenish gold; signed "L.C.T." on both base and shade; matching chimney not signed; Nutmeg burner; shade holder marked "The Twilight"; 12¾ inches high. See. Fig. 587. *Authors' collection.*

Fig. 587. The unassembled Tiffany lamp shown in Fig. 586.

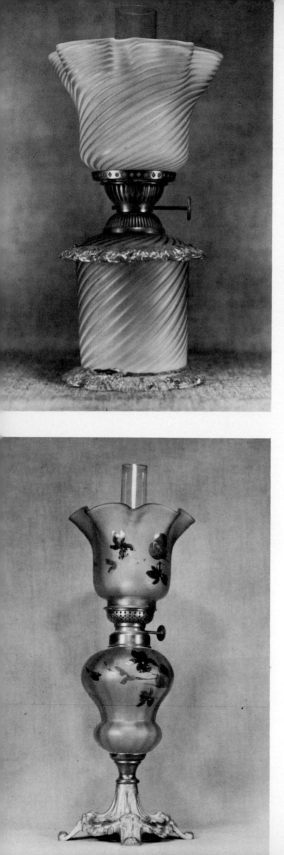

Fig. 588. Satin finish, mother-of-pearl in a ribbed swirl pattern in apricot shading to pink; a row of applied clear glass shells around top and bottom of base; foreign burner; 9½ inches high. *Authors' collection.*

Fig. 589. Brass pedestal base; satin finish, mother-of-pearl in a ribbed swirl pattern; apricot shadings; probably foreign and has a new collar and burner; 10½ inches high. *Bartol collection.*

Fig. 590. Brass pedestal base; green satin glass ornamented with purple flowers and green leaves; "H. & S." on burner; 13 inches high. *Ritter collection.*

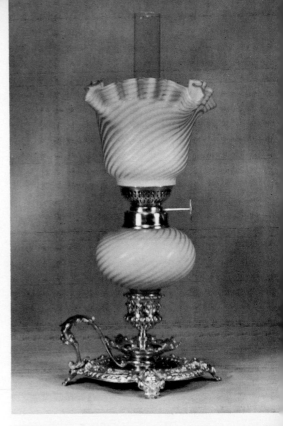

Fig. 591. Silver dolphin pedestal base; satin finish, Diamond pattern mother-of-pearl chartreuse glass; foreign burner; 12 inches high. *Schafer collection.*

Fig. 592. Gold washed base; pink satin mother-of-pearl glass with a ribbed swirl pattern; foreign burner; 11 inches high. *Schafer collection.*

Fig. 593. Brass pedestal base; satin finish mother-of-pearl rainbow glass in Diamond pattern; foreign burner; 10½ inches high. *Schafer collection.*

237

Fig. 594. Rose shading to white mother-of-pearl, satin finish; Diamond pattern; applied frosted shell feet on square base, indented on four sides; foreign burner; 9 inches high. See Fig. 595. *Wehle collection.*

Fig. 595. Apricot shading to light pink mother-of-pearl, satin finish; Diamond pattern; applied clear glass feet on square base, indented on four sides; foreign burner; 9 inches high. Found also in rainbow. See Fig. 594. *Authors' collection.*

Fig. 596. Raspberry mother-of-pearl; Diamond pattern; frosted glass applied feet; foreign burner; 8 inches high. *Schafer collection.*

238

Fig. 597. Embossed blue **satin** mother-of-pearl in Raindrop pattern; Nutmeg burner; 8 inches high. Also found in white. *Luckenbill collection.*

Fig. 598. White satin mother-of-pearl in Raindrop pattern; Acorn burner; 8 inches high. *Authors' collection.*

Fig. 599. *Left:* Raspberry mother-of-pearl, satin finish; Diamond pattern; foreign burner; 5½ inches high. *Right:* Blue satin finish mother-of-pearl; Diamond pattern; foreign burner; 6 inches high. Found also in green and in rose. *Authors' collection.*

Fig. 600. Blue satin mother-of-pearl in Raindrop pattern; applied frosted feet; Nutmeg burner; 8 inches high. *Authors' collection.*

Fig. 601. Pink satin mother-of-pearl in Raindrop pattern; Nutmeg burner; 8½ inches high. Also found in green and blue, both in mother-of-pearl. *Authors' collection.*

Fig. 602. Yellow satin mother-of-pearl in Raindrop pattern; applied frosted feet; Nutmeg burner; 8 inches high. *Authors' collection.*

240

Fig. 603. Yellow satin mother-of-pearl in Raindrop pattern; applied frosted feet; Nutmeg burner; 9¾ inches high. *Authors' collection.*

Fig. 604. Royal Worcester base, cream colored with beige, brown, pink, and blue flowers, green leaves and purple butterfly; shade is etched shaded green to crystal glass; foreign burner; 10½ inches high. *Wehle collection.*

Fig. 605. Amberina base with etched crystal shade; said to be Baccarat; foreign burner; 10¼ inches high. *Schafer collection.*

241

Fig. 606. Pink Baccarat with etched floral cameo design; foreign burner; 11¼ inches high. *Schafer collection.*

Fig. 607. Burmese, decorated with red berries, brown stems and green leaves; unsigned but possibly Mt. Washington Glass Co., New Bedford, Mass.; unmarked burner; 6½ inches high. *Authors' collection.*

Fig. 608. Burmese, signed "Thomas Webb" on base and shade; decorated with flowers and foliage in browns, greens, and delicate yellow; foreign burner; 8½ inches high. *Wehle collection.*

Fig. 609. Hallmark silver base; glossy Burmese shade with pine-cone decorations; foreign burner; 10¼ inches high. *Schafer collection.*

Fig. 610. Signed "Thomas Webb" Burmese; brown and green foliage and red berries decorations; foreign burner; 7½ inches high. *Schafer collection.*

Fig. 611. Cameo lamp; tri-color: white, pink, and citron; said to be Thomas Webb; frosted applied feet; foreign burner; 7¾ inches high. *Schafer collection.*

243

Fig. 612. Stevens and Williams English cameo, white maidenhair fern and butterfly design on cinnamon brown ground; registration number on bottom; English burner; 8 inches high. *Schafer collection.*

Fig. 613. Cased glass hand lamp in dark brown shading to cream color; applied amber handle and vines and pink and white flowers; on burner "The Silver Light Co."; 4 inches high. *Reinert collection.*

Fig. 614. Milk glass base; embossed floral and other decorations; pink flowers and green leaves have fired-on color; 5½ inches high. *Funderwhite collection.*

244

Fig. 615. Porcelain base with pink decorations and blue and red flowers and green leaves; 4¾ inches high. *Reinert collection.*

Fig. 616. Porcelain base in white, pink, and blue; flowers pink and blue; Nutmeg burner; 4 inches high. *Wehle collection.*

Fig. 617. Cameo glass base; white cut to blue; applied frosted thorn feet; 4 inches high. *Wehle collection.*

245

Fig. 618. Bisque swan base in white, green, and beige with gold dots; Nutmeg burner; 4½ inches high. *Rodney collection.*

Fig. 619. Bisque cat base in gray, buff, brown, and other colors; Nutmeg burner; 5 inches high. *Reinert collection.*

Fig. 620. Crown Milano, buff ground with rose in pink, green, and gold; burner marked "J. Dardonville, N.Y."; 4½ inches high. *Authors' collection.*

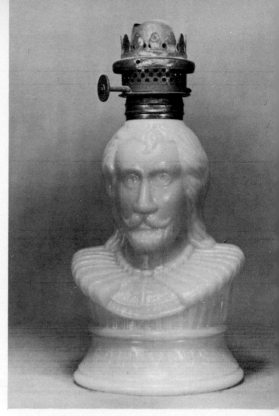

Fig. 621. Blue milk glass house as lamp base; foreign burner; 4 inches high. *Wehle collection.*

Fig. 622. Columbus lamp; pink milk glass; embossed word "Columbus" on bottom of base; shade broken but said to have been umbrella type with embossed ribs matching collar of bust; Nutmeg burner; 5½ inches to top of brass collar. *Funderwhite collection.*

Fig. 623. Porcelain elephant base in buff and brown; foreign burner; 3½ inches high. *Authors' collection.*

247

Fig. 624. Glow lamp (see Fig. 625); here shown unassembled with glass wick holder.

Fig. 625. Glow lamp in ruby glass; marked on base "Glow Night Lamp. No. 0625"; 4½ inches high. A somewhat similar lamp was illustrated in Montgomery Ward & Co. catalog for 1901. It was recommended as giving a soft light with no objectionable fumes. It was said to burn 200 hours with one filling of kerosene. They added: "This little lamp is recommended by leading physicians and is used in nearly all the principal hospitals in the United States." The ruby ones were priced at 50¢ each. See Fig. 624. *Authors' collection.*

248

Fig. 626. Clear glass Glow lamp in ribbed pattern; base marked "Glow Night Lamp. No. 0262. Made in U.S.A. Pat. 5.5.08"; 6¼ inches high. See Fig. 627. *Authors' collection.*

Fig. 627. Glow lamp (see Fig. 626); here shown unassembled with glass wick holder.

Fig. 628. Glow lamp; milk glass with embossed design and painted flowers in red, yellow, and green; pink shading on top of base; 5 inches high. Found also in green glass. *Bartol collection.*

Fig. 629. Fairy lamp; crystal base; Verre Moire (Nailsea) glass shade in butterscotch and white; 5 inches high. This is a typical candle-burning fairy lamp and is included to illustrate the type. *Authors' collection.*

Fig. 630. Vapo-Cresolene lamp; gold gilt iron frame; clear font with embossed "Vapo-Cresolene Use Kerosene"; burner marked "V.C.Co."; 6 inches high to top of iron frame; two types shown. This little lamp is often seen in antique shops. It was actually a vaporizer for a liquid, first marketed about 1879, whose vapors were advertised to have great medicinal value for many serious diseases. See text. The Notices of Judgment of the United States Food and Drug Administration show that when three shipments were seized in 1930 for these false claims and no claimant appeared, the courts issued a "Default decree of condemnation, forfeiture and destruction." This opened the door for the passing of this little lamp. *Authors' collection.*

Patents for Lamp Parts

Between the years 1860 and 1880 close to 1,600 patents were granted for improvements in oil lamps. Many of these improvements were minor and most of them had only a limited sale or were never marketed. Obviously, it is impossible to list all of these patents. We have selected a few which seem most significant or which appear most frequently on miniature lamps.

UNITED STATES PATENT OFFICE.

LEWIS J. ATWOOD, OF WATERBURY, CONN., ASSIGNOR TO THE PLUME & ATWOOD MANUFACTURING COMPANY OF SAME PLACE.

IMPROVEMENT IN LAMPS.

Specification forming part of Letters Patent No. **187,800,** dated February 27, 1877; application filed February 5, 1877.

To all whom it may concern:

Be it known that I, LEWIS J. ATWOOD, of Waterbury, in the county of New Haven and State of Connecticut, have invented an Improvement in Lamps, of which the following is a specification:

Lamps have been made with an air-distributer near the upper end of the wick-tube, and a removable chimney-holder, as in my Patent No. 162,004, and the chimney-holder has been supported by the base or ratchet cap of the lamp, and it has been steadied by a guide within the movable portion of the burner coming against the wick-tube, as in my Patent No. 80,111; but in this latter instance the guide was attached to the removable portion of the burner, and had to be placed over the wick-tube.

In my present invention I make use of an open work guide around the upper part of the wick-tube, permanently attached to the same, in combination with a deflector and chimney-holder attached together, and removable from the other portion of the burner, and with the lower part of the removable portion of a size and shape to fit upon the ratchet-cap or base of the lamp.

By this construction the lamp is more easily kept clean than those heretofore constructed, because the removable portion of the burner can be wiped out, and the perforations around the lower part thereof, and which form the air-distributer, are in the vertical, or nearly vertical, portions of the sheet metal; hence, they do not become obstructed by any carbonaceous accumulation, and the open-work guide that is around the wick-tube is accessible at each side, and hence can be kept clean, and the wick-tube and ratchet-cap are also exposed and easily cleaned.

In the drawing, Figure 1 is a vertical section of the lamp-burner complete. Fig. 2 is a side view of the wick-tube and stationary part of the burner, and Fig. 3 is a plan of the same; and Fig. 4 is an inverted plan of the removable portion of the burner.

The shell *a* of the burner is made with the screw *b* for the collar of the reservoir, and within the same are the wick-tube *c* and wick-raiser *d*. The ratchet-cap *e* covers the wick-raiser, and forms the top of the shell *a*, as usual. The edge of the ratchet cap or shell *a* is adapted to receive the lower part of the removable portion of the burner, and it is preferably cylindrical and made with recesses at *e'*, to receive corresponding projections *i* inside the bottom part of the removable portion of the burner, whereby the latter is properly positioned to the wick-tube. Around the wick-tube *c* there is the open-work guide *f*, that is preferably a disk with perforations, to form a secondary air-distributer, and it is permanently attached to the wick-tube.

The slotted dome or deflector *h* is connected with the chimney-holder *k*, and this is represented with straight sides, round ends, chimney-hooks *l*, and clamping-screw *m*, all similar to those before used; but the cylinder *n*, below the chimney-holder, is adapted to fit upon the periphery of the ratchet-cap, and has the projections *i* aforesaid to enter the recesses *e'*, and determine the proper position of the flame-slot in the deflector in relation to the wick-tube.

The cylinder *n* is preferably perforated with numerous small holes, so as to form an air-distributer.

The parts of the burner are easily kept clean, because access is furnished to both sides of the air-distributer and open-work guide, and when the removable portion of the burner is in place it is firmly supported by the base and guide, and is easily removed therefrom.

I claim as my invention—

The open-work guide *f*, attached to the wick-tube near the upper part thereof, and the shell and ratchet-cap *e*, in combination with the removable portion of the burner, composed of the cone *h*, chimney-holder *k*, and cylinder *n*, substantially as set forth.

Signed by me this 30th day of January, A. D. 1877.

.L. J. ATWOOD.

Witnesses:
GEO. T. PINCKNEY,
CHAS. H. SMITH.

Fig. 1.

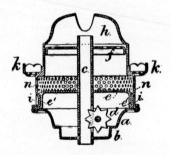

Fig. 2.

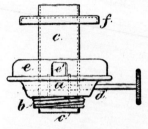

Fig. 4.

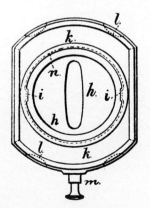

Fig. 3.

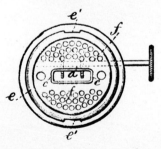

Inventor

Lewis J. Atwood.

per Lemuel W. Serrell

Atty.

Witnesses

Chas. F. Smith
Geo. T. Pinckney

C. W. CAHOON.
Lamp Chimney Holder.

No. 33,824.

Patented Dec. 3, 1861.

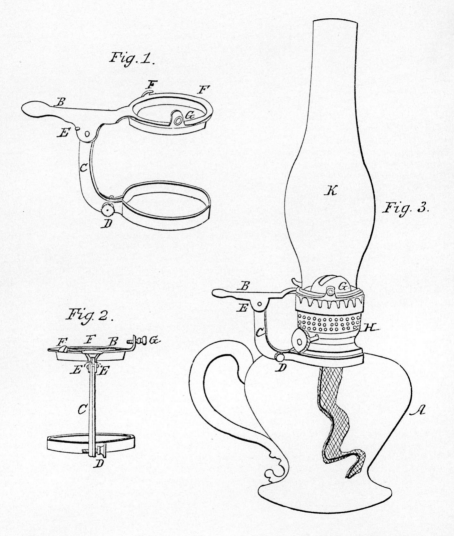

Fig. 1.

Fig. 2.

Fig. 3.

Witnesses.

E. H. Ilsly
James B. Cahoon

Inventor.

Charles W. Cahoon.

UNITED STATES PATENT OFFICE.

CHARLES W. CAHOON, OF PORTLAND, MAINE.

IMPROVEMENT IN LAMPS.

Specification forming part of Letters Patent No. **33,824,** dated December 3, 1861.

To all whom it may concern:

Be it known that I, CHARLES W. CAHOON, of Portland, in the county of Cumberland, in the State of Maine, have invented a new and useful Improvement in Lamps; and I do hereby declare that the following is a full, clear, and exact description thereof, reference being had to the annexed drawings, making a part of this specification, in which—

Figure 1 represents a side view of my improvement. Fig. 2 is a back view of the same. Fig. 3 is a side view of a lamp with the improvement attached.

Similar letters of reference indicate corresponding parts in the three figures.

This invention consists in the novel means employed for attaching to lamps already manufactured and now in use the lever with chimney-fastenings, described in Letters Patent granted to me February 19, 1861; also a stop to prevent the chimney from going too far back. The object is attained by using an adjustable fulcrum in combination with the lever and chimney-fastenings, the adjustable fulcrum having in the back of it indentations constructed and arranged as will be hereinafter fully described.

To enable those skilled in the art to fully understand and construct my invention, I will proceed to describe it.

A represents a common kerosene hand-lamp.

B is a lever.

C is an adjustable fulcrum, constructed of sheet metal, the base of which is made in the form of a part of a circle to fit the collar of the lamp, from which base extend two arms, which are brought nearly together, and are curved so as to reach up and hold the lever B. Near that part of the fulcrum which goes over the collar of the lamp is a screw D, having a head with a shoulder. In that arm of the fulcrum nearest the head of the screw the hole which receives the screw is made larger than the shaft of the screw and has a smooth bore; but the hole in the other arm of the fulcrum is of the proper size to suit the screw and has a thread for it to play in, so that when the screw is turned inward it will draw the arms together, and thus tighten the fulcrum upon the collar of the lamp, keeping it firmly in place, and when turned outward it will loosen it, allowing of its being taken off and placed upon another lamp in case of breakage of the lamp to which it is attached.

E E represent two indentations in the back side of the fulcrum under the lever, and are for the purpose of preventing the chimney from going too far back, which would be an especial liability in lamps without handles.

F F represent two lips, and G is a screw, which are for the purpose of fastening the chimney to the lever.

H is the burner, which is screwed into the lamp in the usual manner.

K is the chimney.

By this improvement a lever with chimney-fastenings is made readily adjustable to lamps already manufactured and now in use, can be adjusted to different lamps, and in case of breakage of the lamp upon which it is placed it can be taken off and attached to another lamp without injuring any of its parts. The indentations in the adjustable fulcrum allow of the distance to which the chimney shall go back, to be regulated without regard to the lamp. If the chimney should go too far back, it might be broken by coming in contact with the stand or table on which the lamp might be placed.

Having thus described a lamp embodying my improvements I deem it proper to state that while I prefer a screw for the purpose of tightening the adjustable fulcrum upon the lamp, yet it is evident that a clasp or movable ring may be used for the purpose, and that while I prefer to attach the adjustable fulcrum to the collar of a lamp, yet where the lamp is constructed to admit of it the adjustable fulcrum may be attached to the burner.

I claim—

1. In combination with a lever and chimney-fastenings, an adjustable fulcrum, substantially as described.

2. In combination with a lever and chimney-fastenings, the indentations F F, for the purpose of preventing the chimney from going too far back, substantially as described.

CHARLES W. CAHOON.

Witnesses:
E. H. ILSLEY,
JAMES B. CAHOON.

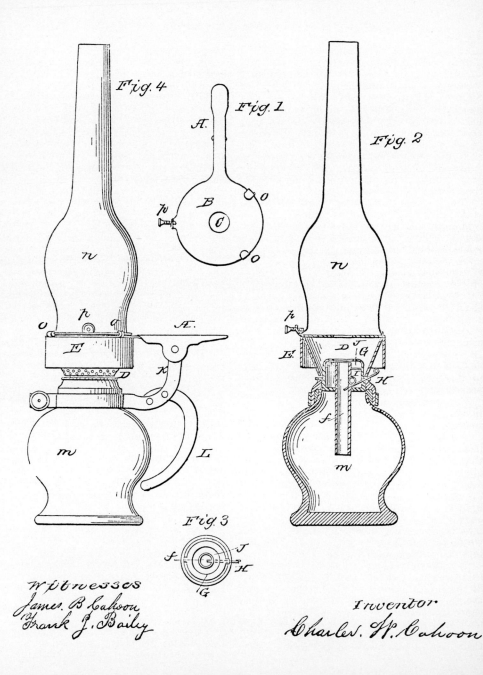

Fig. 4

Fig. 1

Fig. 2

Fig. 3

Witnesses
James B Cahoon
Frank J. Bailey

Inventor
Charles. W. Cahoon

UNITED STATES PATENT OFFICE.

CHARLES W. CAHOON, OF PORTLAND, MAINE.

IMPROVEMENT IN LAMPS.

Specification forming part of Letters Patent No. **33,825,** dated December 3, 1861.

To all whom it may concern:

Be it known that I, CHARLES W. CAHOON, of Portland, in the county of Cumberland and State of Maine, have invented certain new and useful Improvements in Lamps; and I do hereby declare that the following is a full, clear, and exact description of the same, reference being had to the annexed drawings, making a part of this specification, in which—

Figure 1 represents a top view of the lever of the lamp. Fig. 2 represents a vertical section of the lamp. Fig. 3 represents a top view of the lamp-top. Fig. 4 represents a side elevation of the lamp.

Similar letters of reference indicate corresponding parts in all the figures.

This invention consists in improvements upon the lamp for which Letters Patent were granted to me February 19, 1861, the first part of which has reference to the form of the lever for raising the chimney, and its object is to make the lever serve also the purposes of a deflector.

To this end the first part of my invention consists in making that portion of the lever on which the chimney rests in the form of a flat plate, or nearly so, having a circular hole in the central portion of it for the flame to pass through.

The object of the second part of my invention is to make the lighting of the lamp more convenient when a lever is used and an air-chamber. This part of my invention consists in attaching to the lever the air-chamber, so that it will be moved with the lever. In the lamp described in Letters Patent granted to me February 19, 1861, it was necessary to raise the wick above its normal height in order to light it; but by having the deflector and air-chamber attached to the lever and movable with it, it is not necessary thus to raise it, which is a great convenience in lighting one lamp from another.

The object of the third part of my invention is to prevent the wind from causing the lamp to smoke when carried about, when a lamp with a lever and an air-chamber attached thereto is used. This part of my invention consists in attaching to the lever outside of the air-chamber, and at a suitable distance from it to allow the air to pass between it and the air-chamber, a tubular screen.

The object of the fourth part of my invention is to prevent in a measure the flame from smoking when the lever is raised for the purpose of lighting other lamps. This part of my invention consists in placing a flat ring of sheet metal just above the top of the wick-tube and combining the same with a lever for raising the chimney.

The object of the fifth part of my invention is to afford a convenient means for raising a round solid wick when a lamp with a lever for lifting the chimney is used. This part of my invention consists in using a bar having a stop near that end of it which goes into the wick, over which stop is placed a cap attached to the wick-tube and the lamp-top, which has a hole in the outer side of it too small for the stop to get through, yet of sufficient size for the bar to play in easily. Consequently the bar can be moved into or out of the wick and yet be retained in near and convenient proximity thereto.

The object of the sixth part of my invention is to connect with an adjustable fulcrum for holding the lever which raises the chimney a handle, so that in case of breakage of the lamp both the fulcrum and whatever is attached thereto with the handle can be transferred at once to another lamp. This part of my invention consists in attaching to an adjustable fulcrum a piece of metal conveniently formed, which reaches downward from the fulcrum so that it can be easily held by one of the fingers of the hand.

A represents the lever to which the chimney is fastened, and by which it is raised or lowered. It is made of sheet metal, and is pivoted to an adjustable fulcrum K, which fulcrum is fastened by means of a screw to the collar of a lamp *m*.

B represents that part of the lever which is extended to form the deflector, and is in the form of a broad flat plate having a circular hole C in the central portion of it for the flame to issue.

D represents the air-chamber, which is made of sheet metal, and is attached to the lever by means of solder. It is conical in form, and is perforated for the air to pass through, its sides being open at its lower end so that it will go over the wick-tube.

E is a sheet-metal tube without perforations,

and is used for an air-screen. It is attached to the lever by means of solder just outside of the air-chamber D. It is open at the lower end, and being in the form of a straight tube, while the air-chamber is in the form of a cone, space is left between it and the air-chamber for the air to enter the latter. Both the air-chamber and screen may be attached to the lever instead of being soldered thereto by means of thin strips of sheet metal made in the form of hooks which may be riveted to them, allowing the hooks to go over the top of the lever, or holes may be made in both screen and air-chamber, and either straight pieces of wire or thin strips of metal may be inserted into these holes and bent in the form of a hook to hold the air-chamber and screen and then bent over the top of the lever.

f represents the wick-tube of the lamp, which is round.

G is a flat ring made of sheet metal, having two standards, which are attached to the lamp-top by means of solder, and is in such a position that its flat sides are parallel to the top of the wick-tube. This ring is a little larger than the wick-tube and is situated a little distance above it.

H is a bar for moving the wick. It has a stop I near that end of it which goes into the wick.

J is a cap which incloses that part of the bar H on which is the stop, and which holds the bar by means of the stop in close proximity to the wick, but yet allows it to be moved into or out of the wick. This cap is attached by means of solder partly to the wick-tube, serving to cover the slot through which the bar H enters the wick, and partly to the lamp-top, having a hole in its outer side for the bar H to move in, which is too small for the stop on the bar to be got out of. The bar H is made of wire, and the stop I is formed by making a short turn or loop in the wire, so that its two shanks will be longitudinally opposite.

K is an adjustable fulcrum, made of two pieces of sheet metal, which are curved in a circular form, so as to fit the collar of the lamp, and also curved upward to meet the le-ver. They are held together by means of rivets, and are fastened to the collar of the lamp by means of a screw.

L is a piece of metal inserted between the two pieces forming the adjustable fulcrum and fastened thereto by rivets. It is curved downward from the fulcrum, and is intended for a handle to the lamp.

m is the body of the lamp, which is made of glass.

n is the glass chimney, and is fastened to the lever A by means of the two lips *o o* and the screw *p*.

Having thus described my invention, I would further remark that the object of having the deflector in the form of a broad flat plate, or nearly so, is that air may be retained in a measure in contact with a highly-heated surface before it reaches the flame, becoming itself highly heated, and thus producing a more rapid and perfect combustion than by the steep conical deflectors generally in use, when a small wick is used and a small light is desired from oils rich in carbon.

I claim—

1. A lever with chimney-fastenings, having that part of it on which the chimney rests extended so as to form a deflector, substantially as described.

2. The combination of the lever A with the air-chamber D, when the air-chamber is attached to the lever and is movable with it, substantially as described.

3. In combination with a lever for raising the chimney, the air-chamber D and screen E, arranged substantially as described.

4. The ring G, in combination with the lever A, substantially as described.

5. The bar H, having a stop I, in combination with the cap J and lever A, substantially as described.

6. The handle L, in combination with the adjustable fulcrum K and the lever A, substantially as described.

CHARLES W. CAHOON.

Witnesses:
    JAMES B. CAHOON,
    FRANK J. BAILEY.

UNITED STATES PATENT OFFICE.

CHARLES W. CAHOON, OF PORTLAND, MAINE, ASSIGNOR TO JAMES B. CAHOON, OF SAME PLACE.

LAMP.

Specification forming part of Letters Patent No. 31,511, dated February 19, 1861; Reissued August 9, 1864, No. 1,735.

To all whom it may concern:

Be it known that I, CHARLES W. CAHOON, of Portland, in the county of Cumberland and State of Maine, have invented certain new and useful Improvements in Lamps, and that the following is a full, clear, and exact description of the same, reference being had to the accompanying drawing, in which—

Figure 1 represents a side elevation of a hand-lamp embodying all my improvements, Fig. 2 represents a vertical section of the same, Fig. 3 represents a top view of the burner of the lamp, and Fig. 4 a view of the same reversed.

A small lamp, which would burn the oils that are rich in carbon (such for example as kerosene) with success, so as to produce a small quantity of light with economy, and that would be of such light weight and small bulk that it could be readily carried about as a hand-lamp, and would at the same time burn the oil so completely that it could be used for lighting other lamps without smoking, has long been a desideratum, but so far as I am aware of no lamp possessing these qualities has been produced prior to my invention. Hence it is customary at the present day to use candles, small oil lamps, and hand lamps burning explosive, burning fluid, where a small quantity of light is wanted, or the light is to be carried about by the hand, or to be used in lighting other lamps; although it is well known that such means of producing light are much less economical in proportion to the quantity of light given out by them than the large kerosene lamps. In experimenting upon this subject I have found that the same proportionate sizes of wick chimney and thimble, or air cone, which are adapted to produce a perfect combustion in large lamps are wholly unsuited to lamps of small size suitable for hand lamps; and I have found it necessary to make certain new combinations of the elementary constituents of lamps in order to obtain a small hand lamp having all the desirable qualities to which I have before referred. These new combinations constitute my invention, which is divided into several parts.

The object of the first part of my invention is to permit the chimney of the lamp to be withdrawn from the burner and replaced with facility, so that the lamp may be used to light other lamps with despatch by the direct application of its flame.

This part of my invention consists in combining mechanical devices for holding the chimney with a thumb lever, the arrangements of the parts being such that the chimney fastenings are located at one side of the fulcrum of the lever, and a thumb plate at the opposite side.

The object of the second part of my invention is to prevent the accidental contact of the thumb with the hot chimney when removing the latter, whereby a bad burn would be produced.

This part of my invention consists in combining a guard with the thumb lever, the guard being located between the position of thumb and the fastenings for the chimney.

The object of the third part of my invention is to hold the chimney in its place when the lamp is being carried about by hand.

This part of my invention consists in combining a spring with the thumb lever in such manner that the spring bears the part of the lever to which the chimney is fastened upon the burner of the lamp, or its equivalent for sustaining the chimney.

The object of the fourth part of my invention is to protect the chimney from injury by collision with other objects, without interfering with the ready withdrawal of it from the burner, and its replacement thereon.

This part of my invention consists in combining a chimney - guard with the thumb lever, so that the guard, chimney, and lever maintain their proper relations in all positions of the chimney.

It is well known that a lamp body wholly of glass is objectionable on account of its fragility unless it be made of great thickness, and such a glass body is objectionable on account of its weight and cost; on the other hand a lamp body wholly of metal, although free from the defects of a glass body, is opaque and does not permit the user to see the level of the oil within it.

The object of the fifth part of my invention is to enable the user to see when a lamp made of opaque material, such as metal, requires to be filled, without the necessity of unscrewing or removing any portion thereof to permit the user to look into the lamp.

This part of my invention consists in combining a transparent plate with a metal lamp body, so that the combined strength and lightness of sheet metal may be made available for the construction of the greater portion of the body of a lamp, without preventing the user from seeing the level of the oil, and the glass used may be reduced to so small a breadth that it may be made strong enough to resist all ordinary accidents without any material increase in the weight or cost of the lamp.

All the parts of my invention are embodied in the hand-lamp represented in the annexed drawing, and I believe that the best hand-lamp will be obtained by such a use of my invention, although parts of it may be used without the remaining parts as constructors of lamps may deem expedient.

The body A of the hand-lamp represented in the drawing is made mainly of tin plate with a glass plate b inserted in its side. This glass plate is held in place by a frame-work of tin plate, which is soldered to the body, and whose lips a a lap over the edges of the glass plate. The joint is made tight by means of cement, which, when kerosene or oil is burned, may be made of shellac and alcohol. The lamp body has a handle B secured to one side in a convenient position to be grasped by the hand of the user when the lamp is to be moved; this handle also supports the fulcrum pin i of the thumb lever C, to which the chimney D is fastened.

The body of the lamp is surmounted by the burner, which consists of the wick holder g and the thimble or air cone h, by which air is guided against the flame. The wick holder, or tube, g, is secured in a plate j, which is screwed into a tubular head k, that is made fast to the body of the lamp; so that the burner can be removed for the purpose of filling the lamp with oil or supplying a new wick. The wick holder is flat and narrow, or in other words of small breadth, so as to hold a narrow flat wick; and it is fitted with a toothed spindle or barrel m, having a stem and milled head l, by turning which the wick may be raised or depressed. The tube plate j supports the thimble h which surrounds the wick tube, and is perforated at its sides to admit air. The upper end of this thimble is contracted so as to form a circular opening n, that is at a short distance above the upper end of the wick tube and forms the orifice through which the flame issues. The parts of this circular orifice which are opposite the narrow sides of the wick tube are notched, as shown in the drawing, the practical effect of which is to cause the flame to spread laterally.

The lamp represented in the drawings is fitted with a supplementary wick holder for the purpose of holding a supplementary wick.

The supplementary wick holder is located in this instance wholly beneath the tube plate j, and consists of a spring plate c, which holds the upper end of the supplementary wick, p, in contact with the burning wick, q; the side of the wick tube adjacent to the supplementary wick holder is removed, so that no obstacle intervenes between the two wicks; hence the oil drawn up by the supplementary wick is transferred by capillary attraction to the burning wick when the latter is too short to reach down into the oil and draw its own supply.

The burner is surmounted by the thumb lever C, and chimney D. The former is pivoted near the middle of its length to the handle B of the lamp; that portion of it which extends over the handle is formed into a thumb plate d, to which the thumb of the hand that grasps the handle can be readily applied. The portion of the lever which extends over the burner has the form of a broad ring r, that fits upon and is sustained by the conical end of the thimble h; this ring supports the chimney D, which is fastened to the thumb lever by means of two lip fastenings s s, and by a screw t. The thumb lever also sustains the chimney-guard, which consists of a series of wires e, which, being secured by their lower extremities to the thumb lever, project upward at the sides of the chimney, and are connected at their upper extremities by a ring w, that encircles the upper end of the chimney. From this combination of the chimney-fastenings with a thumb lever, the chimney can be readily withdrawn from the burner by the pressure of the thumb, thus permitting the flame that issues from the burner to be brought into contact with the wicks of other lamps, or with gas issuing from gas burners, for the purpose of lighting them; and the chimney can be as readily replaced upon the burner by relaxing the pressure of the thumb.

In order to maintain the chimney in its position when the lamp is carried about by the hand, the ring r, to which the chimney is fastened, is pressed upon the burner by a spring v, located between the thumb plate d and the handle; and in order to prevent the accidental burning of the thumb of the user by contact with the highly heated chimney, a guard-plate, x, is combined with the thumb lever at a point intermediate between the thumb plate d and the chimney D. The combination of the chimney-guard with the thumb-lever permits it to maintain its proper relation to the chimney in whatever position the latter be placed, thus enabling a chimney-guard to be used upon a small lamp adapted to lighting other lamps.

Having thus described a hand-lamp embodying all my improvements, I deem it proper to state that parts thereof may be modified without changing the principle of

C. W. CAHOON.
Lamp Chimney Holder.

No. 31,511.

Patented Feb. 19, 1861.

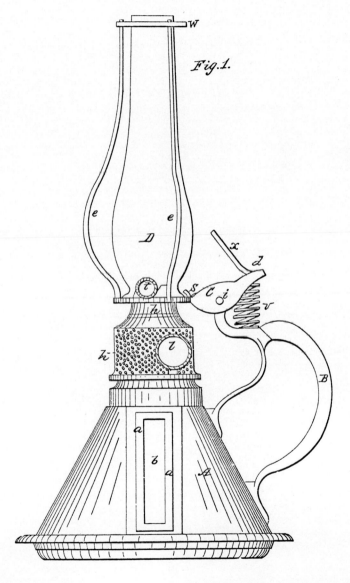

Fig.1.

Witnesses:

A. E. Furbish

Clinton Furbish

Inventor:

Charles W. Cahoon

C. W. CAHOON.
Lamp Chimney Holder.

No. 31,511.   Patented Feb. 19, 1861.

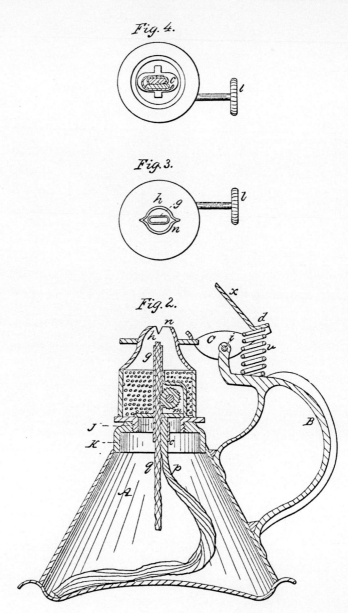

Fig. 4.

Fig. 3.

Fig. 2.

Witnesses:
A. K. F. Furbish
Clinton Furbish

Inventor:
Charles W. Cahoon

my invention; thus for example the precise form of the orifice of the air thimble may be varied, and it may even be rectangular, but its proportionate size to the wick can not be varied materially without rendering the lamp practically valueless.

The practical success of my lamp depends upon the employment of a narrow flat wick, as the object is to afford only a comparatively small light with a perfect combustion of the oil, and I have found by experiment that the width of the orifice of the thimble measured in a direction crosswise to the breadth of the flat wick, or in other words in the direction of the line z z of Fig. 3, should be about as great as the breadth of the wick tube measured in the direction of the line y y of Fig. 3, or even still greater than the breadth of the flat wick tube when a still narrower wick than that represented in the drawing is used, in order to prevent the draft of air from extinguishing the light when the wick is being turned down (after lighting the lamp) to its proper position for burning, and in order also that the flame may extend up through the orifice when the chimney is withdrawn. I have also described the lever for operating the chimney as a thumb lever, from its movement by the thumb of the user; but it is evident that it may be operated by one of the fingers of the user and may be modified to adapt it to such operation.

The lamp represented in the drawings is adapted to burning pure kerosene oil which has not been affected by long exposure to the air; it is well known among dealers that oil which has been so exposed is not as good as that which has been kept from contact with the air, and is liable to smoke when burning.

I do not claim any one of the separate elements, which are combined to make my new combinations, separately; but

What I claim as my invention and desire to secure by Letters Patent is—

1. The combination of chimney-fastenings with a thumb lever substantially as described, so that the chimney may be withdrawn by pressure upon the lever.

2. The combination of a guard with the thumb lever, the said guard being located between the chimney and that end of the lever to which pressure is applied, substantially as described.

3. The combination of a spring with a thumb lever fitted with chimney fastenings substantially as described.

4. The combination of a chimney-guard with a thumb lever, substantially as described.

5. The combination of an opaque lamp body with a transparent plate substantially as described.

In testimony whereof I have hereunto subscribed my name.

CHARLES W. CAHOON.

Witnesses:
CLINTON FURBISH,
A. H. F. FURBISH.

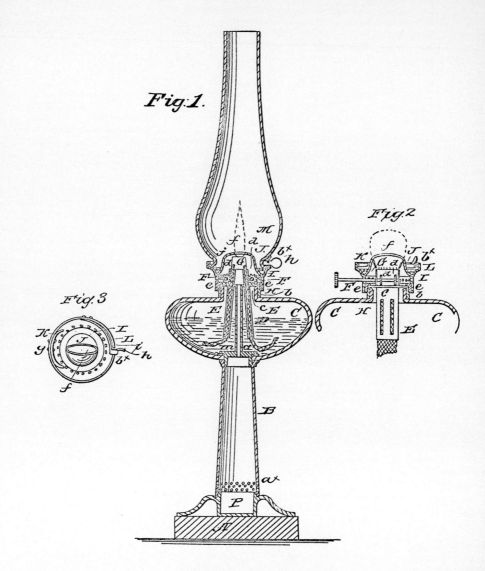

Fig.1

Fig.2

Fig.3

UNITED STATES PATENT OFFICE.

W. H. TOPHAM, OF NEW BEDFORD, MASSACHUSETTS.

LAMP.

Specification of Letters Patent No. 31,496, dated February 19, 1861.

To all whom it may concern:

Be it known that I, W. H. TOPHAM, of New Bedford, in the county of Bristol and State of Massachusetts, have invented a new and Improved Lamp Designed Chiefly for Burning Whale-Oil; and I do hereby declare that the following is a full, clear, and exact description of the same, reference being had to the annexed drawings, making a part of this specification, in which—

Figure 1, is a vertical central section of a lamp constructed according to my invention. Fig. 2, a vertical central section of the lamp top the plane of section being at right angles to that of Fig. 1. Fig. 3, a plan or top view of the lamp top.

Similar letters of reference indicate corresponding parts in the several figures.

To enable those skilled in the art to fully understand and construct my invention I will proceed to describe it.

A, represents the base of a lamp on which a hollow pedestal B, is placed and secured in any proper manner. The lower part of the pedestal B, is perforated as shown at a^x, and on its upper end the body or fountain C, of the lamp is placed—the latter having no communication with the former.

Into the upper end of the pedestal B, there is screwed a head a, to which a flat copper tube D, is attached, the tube D, communicating with the pedestal B, and extending upward as high as the top of a metal band b, which is fitted on the fountain C, and around its orifice as shown in Figs. 1, and 2.

The lower part of the head a just above its screw thread that enters the pedestal B is provided with a flange m and when the head a is screwed into the pedestal B, said flange m rests upon the inner surface of the fountain C. The edges of the fountain are thus clamped between the upper end of the pedestal B and the flange m; a suitable packing i is placed under the flange m to prevent the possibility of leakage. The usual mode of uniting the glass fountains to the pedestal is by cementing.

My improved mode permits the convenient opening and separation of the fountain from the pedestal for cleaning, and at the same time serves as a firm and durable mode of uniting the parts.

E, E, are wick tubes of flat form and secured near their upper ends in a circular plate c, which rests on the band b. The wick tubes are not parallel with each other their upper ends being nearer together than their lower ends. The wick tubes are at opposite sides of the flat tube D, the latter having a central position between the former. Each wick tube E, is slotted at its outer side near its top to receive serrated wheels d, d, which are on shafts F, F, there being one shaft to each wick tube and two serrated wheels on each shaft. The wheels d, when turned or rotated raise and lower the wicks.

To the sides of the wick tubes E, E, there are attached plates G, G, which are slightly curved above the tubes E, and extend from the plate c, to the top of the cone or deflector hereinafter described and close the space between the tubes E, E, above plate c.

The circular plate c, is fitted within a socket or thimble H, which screws on the band b, and secures the plate c, down on the band the upper part of the socket or thimble being provided with a flanch e, which projects over the edge of plate c, as shown in Figs. 1 and 2.

I, is the cap the lower end of which is fitted to the socket or thimble H, by simply sliding over the same. This cap I, is provided with a cone or deflector J, slotted as usual at f, the slot being over the tops of the wick tubes E, E. The cap is perforated as usual to admit air to the flames, both within and at the outer side of its cone J, and the plates G, extend to the ends of the slot f, as shown in Fig. 2.

From the above description it will be seen that the air which feeds the flame passes through the perforations a^x, at the lower end of the pedestal B, and through the flat copper tube D, and impinges against the inner sides of the flames of the two wicks E, E. The air in passing through the tube D, is heated the tube being warmed by the flames, and the tube being of copper readily receives the heat therefrom. The plates G, G, prevent the air coming in contact with the edges of the flame below the cap I—and the flame is consequently allowed to spread the full length of the slot f. Were the plates G, not employed impinging air at the edges of the flame would prevent the flames spreading and their width would be very contracted and broad flames only obtained by using large wicks. The office of the plates G, will be fully understood by referring to Fig. 2, in which it will be seen that the edges of the flames, or one of them rather, is in contact with the plates G, G.

The flat tube D, prevents the wick tubes E, E, being turned in the body or fountain C, and hence the necessity for the socket or thimble II, which admits of the wick tubes being firmly secured in position, without being turned as hitherto required in ordinary arrangements in order that the plate in which they are secured may be screwed into a socket at the orifice of the lamp fountain.

In the cap I, at its upper part there is secured a curved metal plate K, the ends of which project inward toward the center of the cap. This plate is elastic so that its ends may yield or give, the plate being attached at its center to the cap as shown at g, so as to form a double spring. There is also attached to the inner side of the cap a spring L, the disengaged end of which projects inward toward the center of cap I. To this end of the spring a thumb-piece h, is attached with thumb-piece projects through a slot i, in the edge of the cap.

The springs K, L, secure the chimney M, to the cap, the springs fitting over the flanch j, at the lower end of the chimney. The lower edges of the spring K, are rounded in order that they may fit snugly on the flanch, and act efficiently against it. The same springs will serve for different sized chimneys and also allow for the expansion of the same by the heat of the flame. To the outer end of the spring L, there is attached an inclined plate b^x, which admits of the ready fitting of the chimney in its place. The chimney is released by shoving out the spring L, the thumb acting against thumb piece h.

I would remark that the copper tube D, serves by conducting heat down into the fountain C, to render the oil therein fluid so that it may readily pass up the wicks. I would also remark that the tube D, being much smaller than the pedestal B, the latter serves as an air chamber and insures a uniform current of air up through D, preventing the smoking of the flame when the lamp is moved. The elasticity of the column of air contained within B and the interposition of said column between the air entrance at a^x and the discharge at D together with the greater bulk of the air column in B over the area of the tube D, insures a regular supply of air to the flame and consequently a steady and brilliant combustion. The pedestal B, unscrews a short distance above the base A, and there is a chamber P below to receive any oil that may chance to pass into the upper end of tube D.

I do not claim the two wick tubes E, E, nor do I claim irrespective of the arrangement herein shown, admitting air to the flame through a hollow pedestal. Nor do I claim broadly the use of springs for attaching chimneys to lamps.

I do claim as new and desire to secure by Letters Patent—

1. The arrangement of the flanched screw socket H and disk c with the band b tubes D, E, F and cap I in the manner and for the purposes herein shown and described.

2. The employment of the double armed spring K in combination with the cap I and spring L in the particular manner herein shown and described, for the purposes set forth.

3. The arrangement of the rings or plates G to extend from the plate c to the inner surface of the cone or deflector J so as to inclose the flame, all in the manner and for the purpose herein shown and described.

WM. H. TOPHAM.

Witnesses:
    CHARLES C. DUNBAR,
    C. DAVENPORT.

G. W. BROWN.

LAMP-COLLARS.

No. 175,022. Patented March 21, 1876.

Fig. 1.

Fig. 2.

Witnesses
John Becker.
Fred. Haynes

George W. Brown
by his Attorneys
Brown & Allen

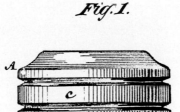

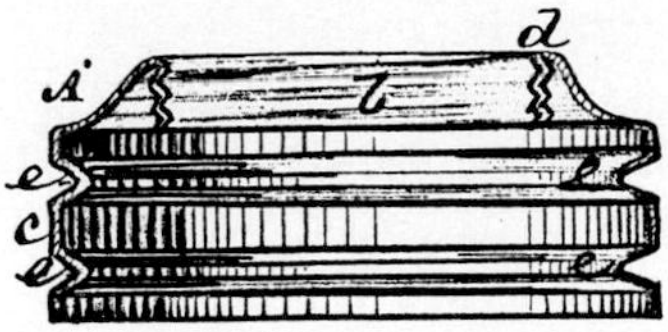

UNITED STATES PATENT OFFICE

GEORGE W. BROWN, OF FORESTVILLE, ASSIGNOR TO THE BRISTOL BRASS AND CLOCK COMPANY, OF BRISTOL, CONNECTICUT.

IMPROVEMENT IN LAMP-COLLARS.

Specification forming part of Letters Patent No. **175,022**, dated March 21, 1876; application filed February 9, 1876.

To all whom it may concern:

Be it known that I, GEORGE W. BROWN, of Forestville, in the county of Hartford and State of Connecticut, have invented a new and useful Improvement in Lamp-Collars; and I do hereby declare that the following is a full, clear, and exact description of the same, reference being had to the accompanying drawing, which forms part of this specification:

To economize metal in the construction of lamp-collars—that is, to make them of as thin sheet metal as possible—so that in the manufacture of such articles by the thousand or million there will be a material saving in expense, it has been proposed to form the screw-thread within their necks or open tops by spinning, swaging, striking up, or other analogous operations, as distinguished from cutting said thread by means of a tap or otherwise, and which cutting of the thread requires a much stouter grade of metal to be used, thereby adding to the expense, and even then giving a less prominent screw-thread than by spinning, swaging, or striking it up out of thinner sheet metal. Thus, among other methods of making lamp-collars out of very thin sheet metal, and at the same time of providing for a bold or well-defined screw-thread therein, is that described in the patent of Frank Rhind, issued June 22, 1875, in which a recessed block, divided dies, and an operating wedge are used for stamping the screw-thread in the metal collar; also, the method described in the patent of Alvin Taplin, issued April 13, 1875, in which the blank out of which the collar is formed is threaded in the flat and afterward struck up into its final or ring form.

Both of these methods are practicable, and admit of the collars being made of very light or thin sheet metal, and so that the collar presents a bold or well-defined interior screw-thread, but while the gaining of these advantages has been a great desideratum, there has been a great disadvantage involved in the use of very light metal, inasmuch as said collar is so limber and weak in its outer portion that it is easily injured, or its form destroyed so as to materially impair its efficiency.

My invention obviates this defect, and at the same time preserves the economy of making the lamp-collar of very thin sheet metal by spinning, swaging, striking up, or otherwise analogously forming, as distinguished from cutting, as by a tap, the screw-thread therein, and consists in a lamp-collar having its interior screw-thread thus formed, and with its body or outer portion stiffened by means of circumferential ridges formed by throwing the metal up or in from the opposite side in the form of a groove, thus giving the collar all the advantage of one formed of thicker sheet metal, likewise contributing to its more perfect retention by the plaster ordinarily employed to hold it on the lamp, and giving a better finger-hold for its adjustment.

In the accompany drawing, Figure 1 represents a side view of my improved lamp-collar, and Fig. 2 a vertical section of the same.

A is the collar, which may be spun or struck up out of thin sheet metal, and the screw-thread *b*, within its upper open portion *d*, formed by spinning, swaging, or striking up, or other analogous process, as, for instance, by threading the collar blank in the flat and afterward striking up such threaded portion into its required ring shape, as in the patent of Alvin Taplin, hereinbefore referred to. Such thin metal lamp-collar, with its well-defined screw-thread, I give all the desired rigidity to, even though using a thinner metal than usual, by forming its body or outer portion *c* with circumferential ridges *e*, produced by throwing the metal up or in from the opposite side in the form of a groove. This may be done by putting the collar in an expanding chuck in a lathe and applying a knurling tool or tools to its body *c*, or it may be done by any other suitable means, and the ridges *e* either be arranged to project internally or externally. The ridges or projections *e*, thus formed in the body *c*, also serve to give a better hold of the collar on the plaster by which it is secured to the lamp.

In this way or by these means I produce a lamp-collar which, while preserving its form and admitting of being securely retained to its place, may be made lighter and cheaper than other collars for the same purpose.

I am aware that lamp-collars having spiral screw-threads stamped in the metal, for the purpose of fitting over a similar thread on the neck of the lamp is old; but this I do not claim.

I claim—

As a new article of manufacture, a lamp-collar constructed of thin sheet metal, with a series of annular circumferential strengthen-ing-ridges, a, curved shoulder d at the top, and screw-threaded flange b, projecting downwardly from the shoulder into the collar, substantially as described.

GEO. W. BROWN.

Witnesses:
    BENJAMIN W. HOFFMAN,
    FRED. HAYNES.

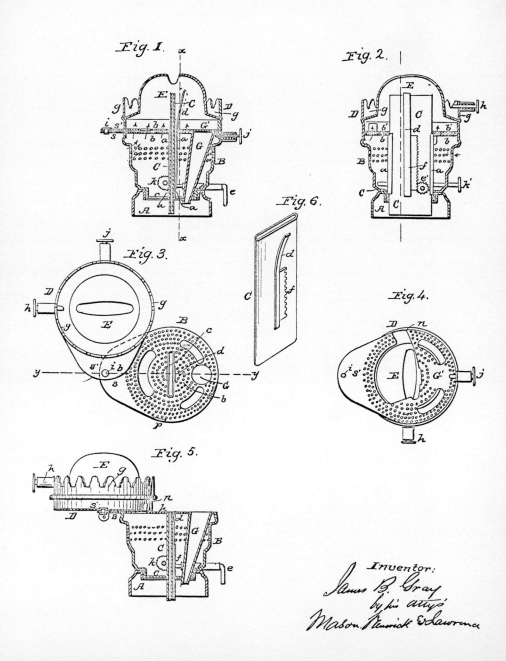

Fig. 1.

Fig. 2.

Fig. 3.

Fig. 6.

Fig. 4.

Fig. 5.

Inventor:

James B. Gray

by his atty's

Mason, Fenwick & Lawrence

UNITED STATES PATENT OFFICE.

JAMES B. GRAY, OF HUDSON, WISCONSIN.

IMPROVEMENT IN LAMP-BURNERS.

Specification forming part of Letters Patent No. **38,960**, dated June 23, 1863.

To all whom it may concern:

Be it known that I, JAMES B. GRAY, of Hudson, St. Croix county, and State of Wisconsin, have invented a new and useful Improvement in Lamp-Burners; and I do hereby declare that the following is a full, clear, and exact description thereof, reference being had to the accompanying drawings, making a part of this specification, in which—

Figure 1 is a vertical diametrical section through the improved lamp-cap. Fig. 2 is a vertical diametrical section taken in the plane indicated by red line $x\,x$, Fig. 1, with the wick-tube elevated. Fig. 3 is a top view of the lamp-cap, showing the wick-tube depressed and the upper portion of the cap moved to one side. Fig. 4 is a bottom view of the hinged portion of the cap. Fig. 5 is a vertical central section, taken through Fig. 3, in the plane indicated by the red line $y\,y$ thereon. Fig. 6 is a perspective view of the adjustable wick-tube.

Similar letters of reference indicate corresponding parts in the several figures.

This invention is intended to enable a person using lamps which have chimneys to them to either trim, fill, or light such lamps without necessitating the removal of the chimneys.

It consists in the combination of a horizontally divided and pivoted lamp-cap with a vertically adjustable wick-tube, which latter, on being depressed to its fullest extent, will allow the upper portion of the lamp-cap to be swung round so as to expose the wick in the upper end of the tube for lighting or trimming it, as will be hereinafter described.

To enable others skilled in the art to make and use my invention, I will proceed to describe its construction and operation.

In the accompanying drawings, A represents the screw-cap, or that portion of the lamp-cap which is cemented permanently to the lamp. B is the lower portion of the divided lamp-cap, which contains and supports the wick-tube C; and D is the upper cone-carrying portion of the cap which is pivoted to the lower portion, B, and supported thereon, as will be hereinafter described. The wick-tube C, which is of the flat kind, is supported in guides $a\,a$, which are secured respectively to the upper horizontal plate, b, and to the lower plate, c, of the cap portion B, and secured to this wick-tube is a hooked friction-spring, d, which

serves the double purpose of preventing the tube C from casually slipping out of position, and also of preventing the tube from dropping down farther than is represented in Fig. 5. The hook on this spring d, in this latter case, catches on the edge of the tube-slot in the plate b, when the tube is depressed to its lowest point. The tube C thus held and supported is operated by means of a thumb-button, e, which is on the end of a short stem that carries on its inner end a spur-wheel, e', which engages with the teeth of a rack, f, affixed to one side of the tube C, as shown in Figs. 2 and 6. It will be seen that by turning e in one direction the tube C will be elevated, and by turning it in the opposite direction this tube will be depressed until its upper end is level with the surface of plate b, which plate is the top of the lower portion, B, of the cap. This portion B is suitably perforated for the admission of air into it, which escapes from it through the perforated plate b, as indicated by the arrows in Figs. 1 and 2, and impinges upon the flame. The upper portion, D, of the cap consists of a plate, b', corresponding in shape and size to the plate b, a cylindrical ornamental rim, g, and a cone, E, which is applied to the rim g in the usual manner of confining cones to lamp-caps. The spring-pin h is intended to confine the chimney to the rim, and this chimney is seldom removed therefrom except for cleaning it. The plate b' is also perforated, as shown in the inverted view Fig. 4, which perforations coincide with those through the plate b when these two plates are fastened in their places, as shown in Figs. 1 and 2. Both plates $b\,b'$ have projections $s\,s'$ formed on them, and these plates are pivoted together at the extreme ends of these projections, as shown at i, which is a vertical pivot-pin. This joint connects the two portions B and D of the cap together, and allows the upper portion with its cone and chimney to be moved round to the position shown in Figs. 3 and 5, thus uncovering the upper plate, b, and exposing the upper end of the wick-tube and the wick. The spring-pin j, which is applied to the movable or hinged portion D, locks this portion in its place when it is in the position shown in Fig. 1. The wick is adjusted in its tube C by means of two wick-spurs, k, one of which is shown in Figs. 1 and 2, which are keyed to a short stem having on its outer end a thumb-button, k'. The spurs k pass through oblong slots in the wick-tube, and when the tube itself is moved the wheels k, with their stem, revolve, and therefore do not displace the wick. When the wick is adjusted by means of these spurs k, the friction-spring d holds the tube, and prevents it from being moved with the wick.

From this description it will be seen that by combining a horizontally divided and hinged lamp-cap with a vertical wick-tube, I am enabled not only to obviate the necessity of removing the chimney from the lamp-cap to light or to trim the lamp, but I can also adjust the wick in the tube, and adjust both wick and tube together, for obtaining the proper position of the same with reference to the opening in the cone E, and thus regulating the intensity of the light and the height of the flame. In short, this combination makes the horizontally-divided lamp-cap practically useful for all kinds of lamps requiring the use of the cone or its equivalent.

When it is desired to obtain access to the wick in my improved lamp-cap, the spring pin j is withdrawn from its catch, and thus released. The upper portion, D, is swung round on its pivot i in the position shown in Figs. 3 and 5. But before this can be done, it is necessary to first depress the wick-tube C until the hook on the upper end of the spring d is stopped by coming in contact with the plate b, when it is known that the wick-tube is in the desired position. The cap portion D can now be moved round, as shown

and described. The wick necessarily projects above the wick-tube a greater or less distance, and to prevent this wick from catching against the rim g, a slot, u, is made in the rim, which slot also extends through the perforated plate b', as shown in Fig. 4, but when the portion D is brought back to its place over the lower portion, B, the projecting lip p, Fig. 3, closes the opening n in the rim.

For filling the lamp without removing the lower portion, B, of the cap, a tube, G, is applied to it, as shown in Figs. 1, 2, and 3, which tube is closed by the blank portion G' left on the plate b', (shown in Figs. 1 and 4,) when the cap D is in place, but when the cap D is swung round the tube G is uncovered.

I am aware that horizontally-divided lamp-caps are not new, nor is the vertically adjustable tube new, when both are separately considered; but

What I claim as new, and desire to secure by Letters Patent, is—

1. The combination of the divided lamp-cap with a vertically-adjustable wick-tube, substantially as and for the purposes herein described.

2. The hooked friction-spring d, or its equivalent, in combination with the adjustable wick-tube and the divided lamp-cap, substantially as described.

JAMES B. GRAY.

Witnesses:
S. H. CLOUGH,
LOU. J. HITZ.

M. B. WRIGHT.
Lamp Burner.

No. 38,999.

Patented June 23, 1863.

Fig. 1.

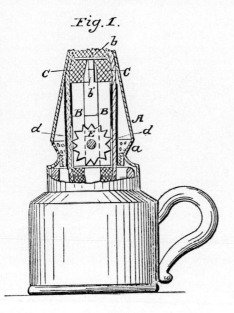

Fig. 3.

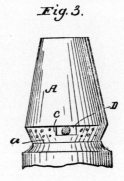

Fig. 2.

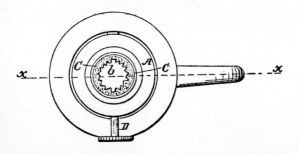

Fig. 4.

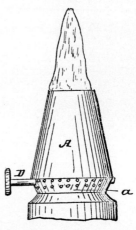

Witnesses:
J. W. Coombs
G. W. Reed

Inventor:
Moses B. Wright
per Munn & Co
attorneys

UNITED STATES PATENT OFFICE.

MOSES B. WRIGHT, OF WEST MERIDEN, CONNECTICUT.

IMPROVEMENT IN LAMP-BURNERS.

Specification forming part of Letters Patent No. **38,999**, dated June 23, 1863.

To all whom it may concern:

Be it known that I, MOSES B. WRIGHT, of West Meriden, in the county of New Haven and State of Connecticut, have invented a new and Improved Lamp-Burner for Burning Coal-Oil; and I do hereby declare that the following is a full, clear, and exact description of the same, reference being had to the accompanying drawings, making a part of this specification, in which —

Figure 1 is a side sectional view of my invention applied to a lamp, *x x*, Fig. 2, indicating the plane of section; Fig. 2, a plan or top view of the same; Figs. 3 and 4, external views of the same.

Similar letters of reference indicate corresponding parts in the several figures.

To enable those skilled in the art to fully understand and construct my invention, I will proceed to describe it.

A represents a conical case or jacket, the lower end of which is attached to a funnel-shaped base, *a*, which is perforated and has two parallel wick-tubes, B B, secured in it, said wick-tubes extending up within the case or jacket about two-thirds or three-quarters of its height. (See Fig. 1.) The upper ends of the wick-tubes are not quite in contact with the inner side of the case or jacket A, a space being left between to admit of a free passage of air all around them and around the wicks for a short distance above the top of the wick-tubes. In the upper part of this case or jacket A there is a circular horizontal plate, *b*, which has its edge serrated or notched, the serrated edge being nearly in contact with the wicks C above the wick-tubes B B. The plate *b* is attached to upright plates *b'*, secured to the inner side of the case or jacket. The wicks C are of the usual flat form, but they are bent or curved nearly in semicircular form, in consequence of the tubes B being of curved form in their horizontal section, and in consequence, also, of the conical form of the case A, with the upper part of which the wicks are brought in contact, as shown clearly in Fig. 1. The lower part of the perforated base *a* of the case or jacket A is screwed into a socket on the top of the lamp, and in said base *a* a shaft, D, is fitted, one bearing of which is an oblong slot, *c*, as shown in Fig. 3, so as to admit of a certain degree of play or vibration of the shaft later-

ally. On this shaft D a serrated wheel, E, is placed, and in line with slots *d d*, made in the inner sides of the wick-tubes. By moving the shaft D laterally the wheel E may be made to engage with either wick, and either of the latter raised or lowered as desired. When the lamp is in use, the wicks C are a trifle above the top of the case or jacket A, and the flame, it will be seen, is supplied with air, which passes up through the case or jacket at both sides of the wicks, the serrated plate *b* causing the air which passes up between the wick-tubes and wicks to impinge against the base of the flame, which is circular in consequence of the wicks being bent each in semicircular form and their edges being in contact.

From the above description it will be seen that the flame is not in contact with the wick-tubes B B, but far above them, with its base in contact with the upper edge of the case or jacket A, and hence the heat from the flame will not be conducted down to the lamp, for, the case or jacket resting on a perforated base, *a*, and the air passing through said base and up through the case or jacket, the heat is absorbed from the latter. Nor can the heat be conducted down to the lamp through the wick-tubes, because the upper end of the tube is surrounded and cooled by the air, and the wicks, just above the wick-tubes, are also surrounded by air. The downward conduction of the heat from the flame is thus prevented. One cause of failure in most burners of this class is the heating of the lamp-body, and the consequent rapid evaporation of the oil and the emission of smoke and a disagreeable odor from the flame.

Having thus described my invention, what I claim as new, and desire to secure by Letters Patent, is—

1. Having the wick-wheel shaft D made to vibrate, substantially as and for the purpose herein shown and described.

2. The combination of the wick-tubes B and wicks C C with the plate *b* and the upper part of the jacket A, substantially in the manner and for the purpose herein shown and described.

MOSES B. WRIGHT.

Witnesses:

DANIEL F. SOUTHWICK,

JOHN. B. STEVENS.

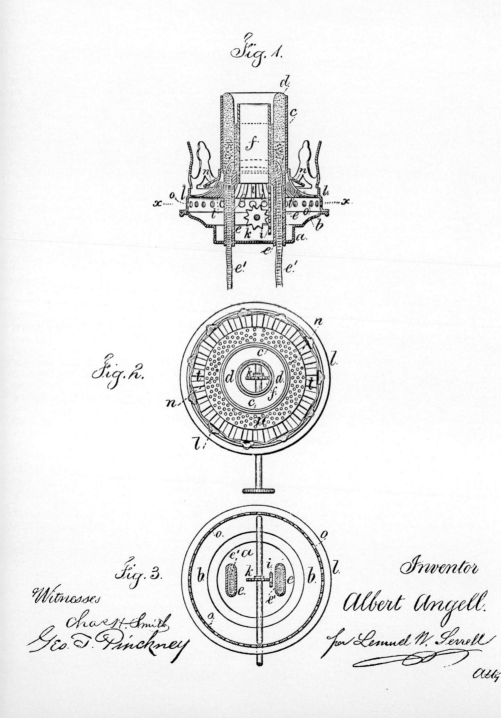

Fig. 1.

Fig. 2.

Fig. 3.

Witnesses
Chas H. Smith
Geo. T. Pinckney

Inventor
Albert Angell.
per Lemuel W. Serrell
Atty

United States Patent Office.

ALBERT ANGELL, OF EAST ORANGE, NEW JERSEY, ASSIGNOR TO CHARLES F. A. HINRICHS, OF BROOKLYN, NEW YORK.

IMPROVEMENT IN LAMP-BURNERS.

Specification forming part of Letters Patent No. **188,490,** dated March 20, 1877; application filed February 5, 1877.

To all whom it may concern:

Be it known that I, ALBERT ANGELL, of East Orange, in the county of Essex and State of New Jersey, have invented an Improvement in Lamp-Burners, of which the following is a specification:

I make use of a cylinder containing a non-combustible wick, and from the bottom of this cylinder there are two or more wick-tubes passing through the body of the lamp to the reservoir.

Within the wick-cylinder there is a movable air-tube, that can be raised or lowered to increase or lessen the flame, and there is a movable chimney-holder and air-distributer around the wick-cylinder.

The object of this construction is to prevent the heat extending down to the reservoir, and to properly regulate the action of the air as it passes up to the flame.

A non-combustible mineral wick has been made in a cylindrical form, and a composition adapted to use as a wick has been employed, and reference is hereby made to Letters Patent Nos. 179,049 and 183,036 for a more full description of such non-combustible mineral wick, and to Letters Patent No. 178,774 for an air-tube that is raised or lowered to regulate the flame.

In the drawing, Figure 1 is a vertical section of the burner. Fig. 2 is a plan of the same, and Fig. 3 is a sectional plan at the line x x.

The screw a is adapted to the reservoir, upon which the burner is to be screwed. This is provided with a disk or burner body, b, upon which rests the removable chimney-holder.

The cylinder c is of a size to receive the composition non-combustible mineral ring d, that forms the Argand wick, and from the bottom of the cylinder c there are two wick-tubes, e e, extending down through the sheet metal of the body within the burner-screw. These tubes contain wicks e', that are led up into the cylinder c, and brought around in opposite directions and secured, so that they cannot pull out accidentally; or a long wick may have a longitudinal slit therein, so that the split portion passes at each side of the central air-tube of the cylinder c, and the ends go down through the wick-tubes.

It is preferable to introduce asbestus, "mineral wool," or similar material between the wick e' and the ring d, of non-combustible material, to prevent the cotton wick becoming charred.

The central movable air-tube f is provided with a rack, i, that is moved by the pinion k upon a horizontal shaft, at the outer end of which there is a button-head. This takes the place of the ordinary wick-raiser, because by lowering the tube f the exposed surface of the mineral wick is increased and the flame enlarged, and by raising the said tube f the flame is lessened.

The removable chimney-holder l is made as a ring, with a conical perforated portion, n, surrounding the wick-cylinder c, and supported by the bars t, and this perforated cone serves to regulate the proportion of air that passes up around the burner and inside the chimney. The perforations at o around the bottom of the chimney-holder serve to regulate the total volume of air admitted to the flame.

It will generally be preferable to employ spring chimney-holders, and to use locking-studs or a bayonet-lock to secure the chimney-holder upon the body of the burner.

I claim as my invention—

1. The cylinder c, receiving the non-combustible Argand wick d, in combination with the wick-tubes e e, passing from such cylinder c down through the metal of the burner, substantially as set forth.

2. The combination, with the non-combustible Argand wick d and movable air-tube f, of the rack i and pinion k, for the purposes and as set forth.

3. In combination with the cylinder c, wick-tubes e, and burner-body b, the removable chimney-holder l, perforated air-distributer n, and perforations o, substantially as set forth.

Signed by me this 25th day of January, A. D. 1877.

ALBERT ANGELL.

Witnesses:
GEO. T. PINCKNEY,
HAROLD SERRELL.

UNITED STATES PATENT OFFICE.

LEVERETT H. OLMSTED, OF BROOKLYN, NEW YORK.

IMPROVEMENT IN LAMPS.

Specification forming part of Letters Patent No. **190,069,** dated April 24, 1877; application filed March 21, 1877.

To all whom it may concern :

Be it known that I, LEVERETT H. OLM-STED, of Brooklyn, in the county of Kings and State of New York, have invented an Improvement in Lamps; and I do hereby declare that the following is a full, clear, and exact description of the same, reference being had to the accompanying drawing, forming part of this specification.

This invention is an improvement on the lamp set forth and shown in my Letters Patent No. 188,533, dated March 20, 1877, and the object of this improvement is to enable the principle of my patented devices aforesaid to be applied to lamps of ordinary construction, thereby effecting great economy and avoidance of waste in the practical application to use of my said patented invention. To this end my present improvements therein comprise a chimney-supporting base provided with arms for supporting the open bottom of the chimney, at or near the top of the wick-tube, and constructed with a flange, fitting within or around the cap of the lamp to retain the base, and consequently the open-bottomed chimney in direct relation with the wick-tube. The invention further comprises a novel combination of a split flange, or equivalent elastic griping device, with the chimney-supporting base, provided with arms for supporting the open-bottomed chimney in the aforesaid relation with the wick-tube, whereby the self adjustment of the base in relation to the cap, and its firmer frictional hold thereon, are provided for.

Figure 1 in the accompanying drawing is a side view of a lamp to which my invention is applied. Fig. 2 is a central vertical section through the wick-tube, cap of lamp, and chimney-supporting base, with a side view of a lamp-chimney, supported by the fingers attached to the chimney-supporting base in relation with the wick-tube, as aforesaid. Fig. 3 is a top view of the wick-tube, chimney-supporting base, and its attached fingers.

A is the collar of the lamp fitted to the oil-chamber B, into which collar is screwed the cap *c,* attached to and supporting the wick-tube *d.*

The chimney is supported by the base *e,* to which are attached the fingers *f.*

In the example of my invention represented the cap *c,* to which the wick-tube *d* is attached, is cup-shaped on its upper side, and the base *e,* which rests on the cap *c,* has a central flange, *g,* fitted to press against the said cap *c.* But the flange may press against the exterior of the said cap, and it may be either continuous, or it may be split vertically to allow the portions separated by the splits, to act as springs against the said cap *c.* The chimney-supporting fingers *f* may be formed of wire or metal strips attached to the base *e,* by riveting or soldering, or they may be struck up from a metal blank, and formed in a single piece with the said base. By these means I supply a very easily made and cheap removable device for supporting the chimney in the desired relation with the top of the wick-tube.

I do not, in this present application, claim a chimney-supporting base having an elastic clamp holding upon the wick-tube of a lamp, and provided with chimney-supporting arms, inasmuch as I propose to apply for separate and distinct Letters Patent thereon; but

What I here claim as my invention is—

1. The flange *g* formed to fit within or around the cap *c,* in combination with the base *e,* provided with the arms *f,* for supporting the open-bottomed chimney with its bottom at or near the top of the wick-tube, substantially as and for the purpose specified.

2. The base *e,* constructed with an elastic flange or like elastic griping device fitting within or around the cap *c,* and provided with arms for sustaining the open-bottomed chimney, substantially as and for the purpose herein set forth.

L. H. OLMSTED.

Witnesses:
  BENJAMIN W. HOFFMAN,
  FRED. HAYNES.

L. H. OLMSTED.
LAMP.

No. 190,069.

Patented April 24, 1877.

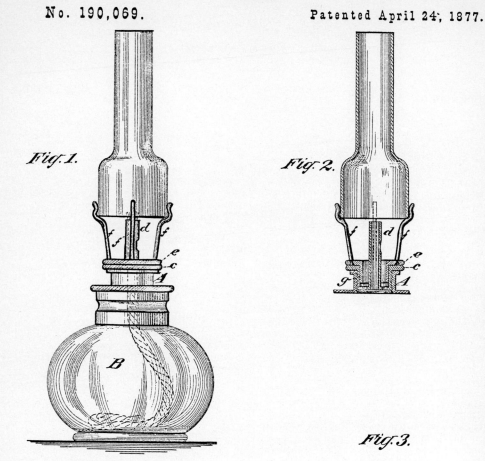

Fig. 1.

Fig. 2.

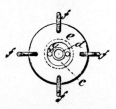

Fig. 3.

Witnesses.
John Becker
Fred. Haynes

L. H. Olmsted
by his Attorneys
Brown & Allen

United States Patent Office.

LEVERETT H. OLMSTED, OF BROOKLYN, NEW YORK.

IMPROVEMENT IN LAMPS.

Specification forming part of Letters Patent No **188,533,** dated March 20, 1877; application filed February 14, 1877.

To all whom it may concern:

Be it known that I, LEVERETT H. OLMSTED, of Brooklyn, in the county of Kings and State of New York, have invented an Improvement in Lamps; and I do hereby declare that the following is a full, clear, and exact description of the same, reference being had to the accompanying drawing, forming part of this specification.

My invention has for its object to supply a larger amount of air to lamps having a small flame, in order to prevent the smell and smoke caused by imperfect combustion in such lamps.

The invention is more particularly applicable to small night-lamps for use in sleeping apartments and rooms for the sick, but it may be applied to larger lamps.

The invention consists in a combination, with the screw-cap of a lamp and the attached wick-tube, of shouldered fingers for supporting the lamp-chimney, which rests upon the shoulders of the said fingers, said shoulders being placed at, or nearly at, a level with the top of the wick-tube, to hold the bottom of the chimney at a height permitting freer access of air to the flame.

This construction permits the flow of air directly to the flame without any obstruction, by perforated or reticulated plates, the feeble upward air-current through the chimney, generated by the low heat of a small flame, being thus rendered sufficient to supply the flame with enough oxygen to prevent the smoke and smell usually resulting from the use of such lamps.

Figure 1 in the drawing is a side view of a night-lamp having my invention thereunto applied. Fig. 2 is a central vertical section through the chimney, wick-tube, and screw-cap of such a lamp. Fig. 3 shows a modification of the invention, and Fig. 4 a detail top view of the chimney-supporting fingers, as applied in Fig. 1.

A represents the body of the lamp; B, the screw-cap; and C the wick-tube attached to the said cap. The wick-tube has a hole, d, formed in its side to admit the point of any instrument for raising and adjusting the wick.

To the connected screw-cap and wick-tube I attach fingers a, having shoulders b formed in or on them, the bottom of the chimney E resting on said shoulders, which are formed in or on the fingers, as nearly as practicable, on a level with the top of the wick-tube C.

The chimney E has its bottom opening entirely unobstructed except by the slender fingers a, and a very feeble upward circulation through the chimney is therefore sufficient to supply the flame with the required oxygen to maintain the proper combustion without smoke or smell.

I claim—

The combination, with the screw-cap, of the chimney-supporting fingers, permanently attached to the wick-tube or other portion of said cap, and holding the lower edge of the chimney up at or about a level with the top of the wick-tube, for the purpose of admitting the greatest possible amount of air to the flame and thus preventing smoking, substantially as herein set forth.

L. H. OLMSTED.

Witnesses:
BENJAMIN W. HOFFMAN,
FRED HAYNES.

L. H. OLMSTED.
LAMP.

No. 188,533.

Patented March 20, 1877.

Fig.1.

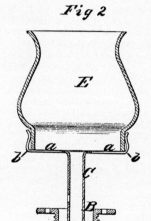

Fig 2

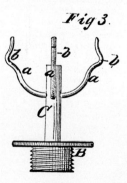

Fig 3.

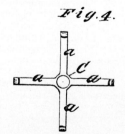

Fig.4.

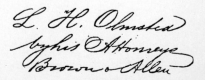

United States Patent Office.

ABRAHAM GESNER, OF WILLIAMSBURG, N. Y., ASSIGNOR, BY MESNE AS-
SIGNMENTS, TO NORTH AMERICAN KEROSENE GAS LIGHT COMPANY.

IMPROVEMENT IN PROCESSES FOR MAKING KEROSENE.

Specification forming part of Letters Patent No. **12,612**, dated March 27, 1855.

To all whom it may concern:

Be it known that I, ABRAHAM GESNER, late of the city and county of New York, now of Williamsburg, in the county of Kings and State of New York, have invented and discovered a new and useful manufacture or composition of matter, being a new liquid hydrocarbon, which I denominate "Kerosene." I obtain this product from petroleum, maltha or soft mineral pitch, asphaltum, bitumen, or bituminous and asphaltic rocks, and shales by dry distillation, and subsequent treatment with powerful reagents and redistillation.

This process, which will presently be described, yields kerosene of three different qualities or proofs, each of which, in my opinion, is a mixture in certain proportions of a spirituous, light, and highly volatile and inflammable liquid with an oily, heavy, and less volatile and inflammable liquid. I have not succeeded in completely separating these liquids in the manufacture, and I see no practically useful object to be gained by doing so. Neither have I ascertained the exact proportions in which the two liquids are mixed; but I suppose the lightest fluid, which I denominate "A" kerosene, to be composed of two parts, by measure, or equivalent proportions of the heavy and eight of the light fluid. Its specific gravity is .750, water being 1, and it boils at 150° Fahrenheit. It is not a solvent of such gums as I have tried to dissolve in it, among which I may mention india-rubber. Sixty-five parts, by measure, of alcohol of specific gravity .844, at a temperature of 60° Fahrenheit, will dissolve thirty-five parts, by measure, of this liquid. By itself the "A" kerosene is highly volatile and inflammable, so much so that even in cold winter weather a good light is produced by forcing a current of atmospheric air through it, circulating the same in pipes, and burning it in jets like gas.

The second, or medium-proof fluid, I call "B" kerosene, and suppose it to be composed of four parts or equivalents of the heavy and six of the light fluid. Its specific gravity is .775 and its boiling-point 250° Fahrenheit. It is not a solvent of gums, but will soften them very slightly. Seventy-five parts of alcohol of specific gravity .844, at a temperature of 60°

Fahrenheit, will dissolve twenty-five parts of this liquid. By itself the "B" kerosene is moderately volatile and inflammable, but will not, like the "A," yield a good light by having a current of air passed through it and burned.

The third, or low-proof fluid, I call "C" kerosene, and suppose it to be composed of six parts or equivalents of the heavy and four of the light liquid. Unlike the "A" and "B," the heavy liquid preponderates in and gives character to the "C" kerosene. Its specific gravity is .800 and its boiling-point is 350° Fahrenheit. Unlike "A" and "B," it is not soluble in alcohol, but is a good solvent of gums, as india-rubber dissolves in it readily. It is not very volatile or inflammable; but in an Argand lamp with a button over the wick it burns with a brilliant white light, without smoke or the naphthalous odor so offensive in many hydrocarbons having some resemblance to this, but possessing very different properties. As burning-fluids for the purpose of artificial illumination, these are highly useful and economical, either separately, mixed together, or "A" and "B" mixed with alcohol. The "C" kerosene has also proved very good as a lubricant for machinery where it has been tried; but, being a new and almost untried thing, the kerosene doubtless has very numerous uses besides its adaptation to illumination and lubrication that will soon be discovered after it is manufactured on the large scale and put into the market as an article of trade. Moreover, as the rocks whence the kerosene is most abundantly obtained are widely disseminated and the deposits of them are of almost unlimited extent, an immense mass of hitherto useless matter will by means of this invention be rendered available for the uses of mankind as a cheap and convenient substitute for illuminating purposes for the oils and fats, which are yearly increasing in scarcity and price.

The process and apparatus I employ in producing the kerosene I will now proceed to describe, premising that I do not confine myself to any particular form or arrangement of apparatus, but intend to use whatever may prove most convenient in any given case.

The first part of the process consists in submitting the raw material to dry distillation at the lowest temperature at which the kerosene will volatilize, care being taken not to raise the temperature so long as tolerably rapid evaporation continues, and the heat must not in any case be raised above 800° Fahrenheit, as the heat if raised to the slightest perceptible red in daylight would be so high as to defeat the whole object of the process, for a greatly-increased production of gas would take place and the liquid produced would be naphtha instead of kerosene. Whatever gas may be generated I employ for illuminating purposes in the ordinary manner, and also as fuel for heating the still. For this dry distillation I have used large cast-iron retorts set in suitable furnaces for the evaporation and metal pipes or chambers surrounded by water for the condensation of the vapor. The liquid products of this distillation are heavy tar and water or ammoniacal liquor, which lie at the bottom of the receiver, and a lighter liquid, which floats above them. The heavy liquids and the light are separated by drawing off one or the other into another vessel by means of a cock, siphon, or otherwise. The heavy liquids may be utilized or disposed of advantageously; but they have no further connection with this process, and therefore I shall not here describe the manner in which I propose to utilize them. The light liquid is then submitted to redistillation, at the lowest possible heat, in a common still and condenser. The product of this redistillation is a light volatile liquid, which accumulates in the receiver, and a heavy tarry residuum left in the still, and which may be added to the heavy liquid impurities of the first distillate. The light liquid is transferred from the receiver to a suitable vessel or vat and mixed thoroughly with from five to ten per cent. of strong sulphuric, nitric, or muriatic acid, according to the quantity of tar present. Seven per cent. is about the average quantity required; but any quantity is useful. I have enumerated three acids; but I give the preference to sulphuric, although either of the others will answer very well. I also mix with the liquid from one to three per cent. of peroxide of manganese, according to the turbidness of the liquid, about two per cent. being the average quantity required. It has the effect of facilitating greatly the precipitation of certain of the impurities which the liquid contains; but, although useful, I do not deem it essential. After these substances have been thoroughly mixed with the liquid by agitation it is allowed to stand from twelve to twenty-four hours without being disturbed, in order that the impurities may subside. The light supernatant liquid is now separated from the impurities, both solid and liquid, that have settled at the bottom of the tank by drawing off either the one or the other into a separate vessel. I next mix the distillate with about two per cent., by weight, of powdered and freshly-calcined lime. The latter, by its powerful affinity for water, will absorb it thoroughly from the liquid hydrocarbon, which always at this stage of the process contains it in greater or less quantity. Lime by its alkaline properties will also neutralize any acid in the liquid. After the lime has been thoroughly mixed with the liquid by stirring, the mixture is again distilled, care being taken to raise the heat gradually and slowly first to about 160° Fahrenheit, where it is kept by regulating the damper until all the vapor has passed over into the receiver that the liquid will yield at this temperature. This product or distillate is the "A" kerosene, and is drawn off from the receiver into an appropriate vessel. The heat is now raised by again drawing the damper to about 260° Fahrenheit, when vapors will again rise and be condensed in the receiver. As soon as the distillate ceases to flow at this temperature it is drawn off from the receiver into a separate vessel, and it constitutes the "B" kerosene. The heat of the still is now raised to about 360° Fahrenheit, when vapors will again rise and condense in the receiver. As soon as the distillate ceases to run at this temperature the process is complete. This last product is the "C" kerosene.

The quantity of lime I have mentioned is the quantity I have found sufficient in all cases; but any quantity less than ten per cent. would be useful. The lime as an alkali appears to exert a specific influence or effect, which is indispensable to the good quality of the product. Neither soda nor potash can produce this effect in any form in which I have tried them, and I have made special and numerous efforts to replace the lime with these alkalies.

To deprive the liquid of water by freshly-calcined lime is important, because, as I have discovered, water is highly injurious to the process and product, even in very small quanties, as it causes carbonic acid to pass over with the distillates, giving to them a creosotic odor, which is extremely offensive. It is one of the great and peculiar advantages of my process that the fluids which it produces have no disagreeable odor.

I claim—

The process herein described for extracting the liquid hydrocarbons, which I have denominated "kerosene," from asphaltum, bitumen, asphaltic and bituminous rocks and shales, petroleum, and maltha by subjecting any of these substances to dry distillation, rectifying the distillate by treating it with acid and freshly-calcined lime, and then submitting it to redistillation, as herein set forth.

In testimony whereof I have hereunto subscribed my name.

ABRAHAM GESNER.

Witnesses:
PETER HANNAY,
P. H. WATSON.

Bibliography

Anonymous, "Miniature Lamps." *Spinning Wheel,* December 1958.

_____, "Novelties in Night Lamps." *Spinning Wheel,* October 1962.

_____, "Miniature Lamps, a Pictorial Study." *Spinning Wheel,* December 1966.

_____, Notices of Judgment 1930-1931 (Food and Drug Cases). Washington.

_____, Patent Records. U.S. Patent Office. Washington.

BARBOUR, HARRIOT BUXTON. *Sandwich the Town that Glass Built.* Boston 1948.

COLE, ANN KILBORN. "Lamps in Miniature." *Philadelphia Inquirer Magazine,* January 24, 1960.

DOZOIS, DOROTHEA ANN. "New Interest in Old Lamps." *Hobbies,* November 1947.

FREEMAN, LARRY. *Light on Old Lamps.* Watkins Glen, N.Y. 1946.

GIDDENS, PAUL H. *Early Days of Oil.* Princeton, N.J. 1948.

HAYWARD, ARTHUR H. *Colonial Lighting.* Boston 1923.

KAMM, MINNIE WATSON. Pitcher Books (Nos. 1-8). Detroit 1939-1954.

LEE, RUTH WEBB. *Sandwich Glass* 8th ed. Northborough, Mass. 1947.

PETERSON, ARTHUR G. *Salt and Salt Shakers.* Washington 1960.

REVI, ALBERT CHRISTIAN. *Nineteenth Century Glass.* New York 1959.

THWING, LEROY. *Flickering Flames. A History of Domestic Lighting Through the Ages.* Rutland, Vt. 1958.

WATKINS, C. MALCOLM. *Artificial Lighting in America 1830-1860* Washington 1951.